YOU WERE MADE FOR GREATNESS!

BY
MaryAnn Diorio, PhD

Dedication

For Dom, my man of steel and velvet ...

YOU WERE MADE FOR GREATNESS!

Discovering God's Will for Your Life

BY

MaryAnn Diorio, PhD

TopNotch Press
Merchantville, New Jersey

Copyright 2011 by MaryAnn Diorio.

All rights reserved. No part of this publication may be reproduced, stored in a retrieval system, or transmitted in any form or by any means—electronic, mechanical, photocopy, recording, or any other—except for brief quotations in printed reviews, without the prior permission of the author and publisher.

Library of Congress Catalog Card Number: 88-70291.

ISBN 0-930037-03-0 Hardcover
ISBN 0-930037-02-2 Softcover

Originally published by DAYSTAR COMMUNICATIONS, Millville, NJ 08332

Second Edition published by TOPNOTCH PRESS, Merchantville, NJ 08109.

Cover design by Robert Ousnamer.

PREFACE TO E-BOOK VERSION

It is with great gratitude to my Lord and Savior Jesus Christ, to Cheryl Cowell, to Robert Ousnamer, and to my wonderful husband Dom that I release this first e-book version of *You Were Made for Greatness*, originally titled *Selling Yourself on You*. This e-book version contains some minor changes better to reflect its new title.

After over 45 years of walking with God the Father, His Son Jesus Christ, and His precious Holy Spirit, I can vouch for the absolute truth of His Holy Word. God means what He says, and He says what He means. We have only to believe what He says and make it the final authority in our lives, above circumstances, medical reports, and financial statements. Only then will we see His Word come to pass in our lives.

Throughout all of my years of seeking, praying, listening, and obeying God, I have learned that He responds not to our need, but to our faith. This may seem strange and heartless on God's part, but the truth is that God is infinitely compassionate and that He already responded to every single one of our needs through the death and resurrection of Jesus Christ. It is our faith in that response that moves His hand on our behalf.

As you read this book, I pray that our Lord will give you a revelation of who you are in Christ. May the eyes of your heart be opened so that you will see and believe the truth that you were, indeed, made for greatness. May you then walk in that truth all the days of your life, for God's glory and for the building of His Kingdom.

MaryAnn Diorio, PhD
Cherry Hill, New Jersey
May 25, 2011

PREFACE TO PRINT UPDATE

It is with great gratitude to my Lord and Savior Jesus Christ and to my wonderful husband Dom that I release this updated print edition of *You Were Made for Greatness*, originally titled *Selling Yourself on You*. This updated version contains some minor changes better to reflect its new title.

After over 45 years of walking with God the Father, His Son Jesus Christ, and His precious Holy Spirit, I can vouch for the absolute truth of His Holy Word. God means what He says, and He says what He means. We have only to believe what He says and make it the final authority in our lives, above circumstances, medical reports, and financial statements. Only then will we see His Word come to pass in our lives.

Throughout all of my years of seeking, praying, listening, and obeying God, I have learned that He responds not to our need, but to our faith. This may seem strange and heartless on God's part, but the truth is that God is infinitely compassionate and that He already responded to every single one of our needs through the death and resurrection of Jesus Christ. It is our faith in that response that moves His hand on our behalf.

As you read this book, I pray that our Lord will give you a revelation of who you are in Christ. May the eyes of your heart be opened so that you will see and believe the truth that you were made for greatness. May you then walk in that truth all the days of your life, for God's glory and for the building of His Kingdom.

MaryAnn Diorio, PhD,
Merchantville, New Jersey
January 1, 2018

Acknowledgments

The making of a book is a team effort, and so it has been with this book as well. So many people have taken part in its shaping that another volume would be required to thank them all. A few have played key roles in its completion. It is these people I would especially like to acknowledge and thank:

The late Pastor Woodson D. Moore of Fairton Christian Center, Fairton, New Jersey, for his faithful and uncompromising teaching of the Word of God;

Mr. Angelo Nardone for his unconditional friendship and support and for his superb insight into human nature;

Mr. John Crowe for showing me by his life what a winner really is;

Mr. Rex Renfrow for not only talking the talk of Christian love, but for walking the walk as well; Mr. Bill Britt for his humility, wisdom, leadership, and strength;

Special thanks are also due to the following:

My late parents, Augustus and Vincenza Genova, for teaching me the meaning of commitment; My sister, the late Rosalind Genova, for her faithfulness in prayer during the writing and publishing of this book;

My sisters, Dolores Miller and Gloria Cappadona, for refreshing me when they were not even aware of doing so;

My former sister-in-law, Amy Sunshine, for generously reading the manuscript and offering encouragement;

My brother, Angelo Genova, Esq., for his inimitable sense of humor;

My brothers, Anthony Genova, Bruno Genova, Esq., and Gino Genova, for revealing to me the unique miracle of each person.

Extra special thanks and appreciation go to my fantastic (now adult) daughters, Dr. Lia C. Gerken and Gina L. Diorio, for enduring pizza for dinner above and beyond the call of duty during their childhood years when I wrote this book; for generously attributing to "genius" a distracted mother whose mind was usually on her book; and for patiently sending "earth-to-mom" signals in order to communicate.

No words can adequately express my deep gratitude to my wonderful husband Dom for his strength, his patience, his understanding, and his love during the writing of this book. Without a word of complaint, he helped me wash dishes, make beds, cook meals, and iron shirts. He encouraged me when the task seemed overwhelming; and he rejoiced with me when it was completed. His great sense of humor during the tough times made all the sacrifices worthwhile. This book is a tribute to his greatness.

Finally, I would like to thank Cheri Cowell and Robert Ousnamer of Living-Parables.com. Their expertise in turning the original print edition of this book into an e-book has been of invaluable help to me and a tremendous answer to prayer.

Above all, I give thanks to my God for using me as His vessel in writing this book and for guiding me to its completion. To Him be all the glory for what He will accomplish through its pages.

Permissions

Scripture quotations marked KJV are taken from the King James Version of the Bible.

Verses marked TLB are taken from *The Living Bible*, copyright 1971 by Tyndale House Publishers, Wheaton, IL. Used by permission.

Scripture quotations marked (AMP) are taken from The Amplified Bible. Old Testament Copyright © 1965, 1987 by The Zondervan Corporation. The Amplified New Testament Copyright © 1958, 1987 by The Lockman Foundation. Used by permission.

Scripture quotations marked (NIV) are from the Holy Bible, New International Version. Copyright © 1973, 1978, 1984 International Bible Society. Used by permission of Zondervan Bible Publishers.

Excerpt from *Prayer Is Invading the Impossible* by Jack Hayford. Copyright © 1977 by Bridge Publishing, Inc. Reprinted by permission of Bridge Publishing, Inc., South Plainfield, NJ 07080.

Excerpt from *The Eagle Christian* by Kenneth Price. Copyright © 1984 by Kenneth L. Price. Used by permission of the author.

Excerpt from *Success: the Glenn Bland Method* by Glenn Bland. Copyright © 1975 by Glenn Bland. Used by permission of Tyndale House Publishers. All rights reserved.

Excerpt from *The Battle in the Heavenlies* by David Nunn. Copyright © n.d. by David Nunn. Used by permission of the author.

Excerpts from *Self-Love: The Dynamic Force of Success* by Robert H. Schuller. Copyright © 1969 by Robert H. Schuller. Reprinted by permission of the publisher, E. P. Dutton, a division of NAL Penguin, Inc.

Excerpts from *Psycho-Cybernetics* (Pocket Books Edition) by Dr. Maxwell Maltz. Copyright © 1960 by Prentice-Hall, Inc. Used by permission of the publisher, Simon & Schuster, New York, NY.

Excerpts from *The Believer's Authority* by Dr. Kenneth Hagin. Copyright © 1984 by RHEMA Bible Church, aka Kenneth Hagin Ministries, Inc. Used by permission of Kenneth Hagin Ministries, Tulsa, Oklahoma.

Excerpts from *The Ultimate Power* by Dave Grant. Copyright © 1983 by Dave Grant. Published by Fleming H. Revell Company. Used by permission.

Excerpt from *Seeds of Greatness* by Denis Waitley. Copyright © 1983 by Denis E. Waitley, Inc. Published by Fleming H. Revell Company. Used by permission.

Excerpt from *See You at the Top* by Zig Ziglar. Copyright © 1975 by Zig Ziglar. Used by permission of the publisher, Pelican Publishing Company, Inc.

Excerpt from *The Art of Loving* by Erich Fromm. First Perennial Library Edition. Copyright © 1956 by Erich Fromm. Used by permission of Harper & Row Publishers, Inc.

Excerpt from *Wilma: The Story of Wilma Rudolph* by Wilma Rudolph. Martin Ratoovsky, Editorial Associate. Copyright © 1977 by Bud Greenspan. Used by permission of NAL, New York, NY.

Excerpt from *The Winner's Edge* by Denis Waitley. Copyright © 1980 by Denis Waitley. Used by permission of the author.

Excerpts from *Positive Imaging* by Norman Vincent Peale. Copyright © 1982 by Norman Vincent Peale. Published by Fleming H. Revell Company. Used by permission.

Excerpt from "Heirs to a Grand Inheritance," *In Touch*™ Magazine, October 1984, by Dr. Charles Stanley. Copyright © 1984. *In Touch*™ Magazine, ITM, Inc. /In Touch Ministries, Atlanta, Georgia. Used by permission.

Table of Contents

Introduction 1
Part I: Grasshoppers and Giants **3**
Chapter One: You Are What You Think You Are 5
Chapter Two: Facts Don't Count! 9
Chapter Three: Psychological Escape-Hatches 15
Chapter Four: Shaping Your Circumstances 23
Part II: The Transformed Mind **29**
Chapter Five: Human Computers 31
Chapter Six: Your Attitude Control Center 41
Chapter Seven: Harnessing Your Thought Power 45
Chapter Eight: The Single Eye 51
Part III: Learning to Love Yourself **59**
Chapter Nine: Accepting Yourself 63
Chapter Ten: Forgiving Yourself 71
Chapter Eleven: Discovering the Real You 73
Chapter Twelve: The Potter and the Clay 83
Part IV: The Power of the Dream **85**
Chapter Thirteen: Catching the Vision 87
Chapter Fourteen: Imagining the Vision 91
Chapter Fifteen: Writing the Vision 101
Chapter Sixteen: Fulfilling the Vision 109
Part V: Choosing To Be A Giant **113**
Chapter Seventeen: The Privilege of Choice 115
Chapter Eighteen: The Responsibility of Choice 119
Chapter Nineteen: The Power of Choice 125
Chapter Twenty: The Fruit of Choice 129
Part VI: The Believer's Authority **135**
Chapter Twenty-One: It's War! 137
Chapter Twenty-Two: Preparing for Battle 143
Chapter Twenty-Three: The Keys of the Kingdom 147
Chapter Twenty-Four: Possessing the Land 151
Part VII: Joint Heirs with Christ **157**
Chapter Twenty-Five: Heaven Is Heir-Conditioned 159
Chapter Twenty-Six: Inheriting the Promises 165
Chapter Twenty-Seven: The Kingdom Is Now 167
Chapter Twenty-Eight: You Are God's Dream 171
About The Author 175
Other Books by Dr. MaryAnn Diorio: 177

Introduction

"God doesn't make junk!" The words of the speaker at the marriage seminar my husband and I were attending resounded throughout the room and pierced my consciousness. Never before had I heard it put so bluntly and so effectively.

In the years that followed, those words would often rise within me. I knew they were true, but I wondered why so many Christians had trouble believing them. As I looked around, it was obvious that most believers were not living the victorious life promised to us in God's Word. Many considered themselves inept, defeated, and unworthy of success. Something was wrong somewhere.

While searching for the causes of this lack of self-esteem among Christians, I discovered the words of Hosea 4: 6 (KJV): "My people are destroyed for lack of knowledge." It became increasingly clear to me that many Christians were living defeated lives because they did not know who they are in Jesus Christ.

I realized that many of us had been listening to lies all of our lives. We had listened so long and so often that we had come to believe those lies.

The Bible tells us that faith comes by hearing and hearing by the Word of God (Romans 10: 17 KJV). One day, as I was meditating on this verse, the first part of it struck me: faith comes by hearing. In one of those special moments of revelation, I saw that faith in anything comes by hearing. If you hear something long enough, you will begin to believe it whether or not it is true.

But just because your mother may have called you "stupid" when you were six years old doesn't mean that you are. Or just because your father may have complained that you would never amount to anything after you failed your math course doesn't mean that you won't. YOU choose whether you will fail or succeed in life. YOU are the deciding factor.

During the past several years, I have counseled Christians with all kinds of problems. Repeatedly, I found that their problems stemmed from a poor self-image. This troubled me because Christians, of all people, should be confident, poised, and in control.

While the causes of a low self-image are varied, the effects of it in one's life share a common denominator: a poor self-image prevents you from being an effective witness for Christ and from fulfilling God's dream for your life.

There is no need for poor self-esteem among Christians. God has made us more than conquerors through Christ. How, then, can we overcome feelings of inferiority and be all that God wants us to be? The answer lies in His Word.

The purpose of this book is to show you from the Scriptures how truly precious and important you are. Primarily a self-help book, it will give you practical guidelines to aid you in overcoming a poor self-image. Whether or not you suffer from a lack of self-esteem, this book will help you better to understand the negative forces working to pull you down. It will also show you how you can take control of those forces and lead a more satisfying and productive life.

When you discover who you really are in Christ, you will experience a new dimension of living you never dreamed possible. I encourage you to read this book with an open mind and an open heart. As you move through its pages, may you catch the vision of God's love for you and of your greatness and unlimited potential in His Son, Jesus Christ.

Part I

Grasshoppers and Giants

You are special! No one else has your fingerprints, your voice, your smile, your laugh. There is only one you. You are not an accident, as some would have you believe. The Bible says that God knew you even before He created you. He made all the delicate, inner parts of your body and knit them together in your mother's womb. You are "wonderfully complex!" (Psalm 139: 13-14 TLB).

Just consider that any number of genetic combinations could have occurred at the moment of your conception. Yet God wanted that particular, unique combination to occur which produced you.

God knows everything about you. He even knows the number of hairs on your head.

Because God made you, He cares about every detail of your life. Those of us who are parents know how involved we get with our children. We want them to succeed spiritually, physically, academically, and socially. God's desire to see His children succeed is even greater than ours as parents, for God's love is infinite whereas our love is finite.

The humanistic philosophy prevalent in the world today teaches that man is of little importance and that his presence on this earth is simply the result of chance. This philosophy discounts the uniqueness of man and renders him nothing more than a collection of molecules destined to annihilation.

It is no wonder that this kind of thinking robs human life of its intrinsic value and results in the horrors of abortion, infanticide, and euthanasia. Man is NOT the measure of all things, as the humanists proclaim. GOD is the measure of all things.

Chapter One

You Are What You Think You Are

How do you see yourself? Do you really believe God's promise that through Christ you can do all things (Philippians 4: 13)? Or do you get a sinking feeling in your stomach that maybe that promise was meant for someone else?

More often than not, how you see yourself is how others see you. You are what you think you are, and you will act according to what you believe about yourself.

Many Christians suffer from what I call a "grasshopper complex." This is an inferiority complex whose root cause is a lack of knowledge of who we are in Christ.

Let's take a look at a Scripture passage that describes the "grasshopper complex."

God had instructed Moses to lead the Israelites into the Promised Land. Just before reaching it, Moses sent spies to investigate the territory. They were to determine what the people were like, how large the population was, what cities and villages there were, and whether they were fortified.

After forty days of scouting, the spies returned with a negative report: "The land is full of warriors, the people are powerfully built, and we saw some of the Anakim there, descendants of the ancient race of giants. We felt like grasshoppers before them, they were so tall!" (Numbers 13: 32-33 TLB).

The report of the spies caused fear and rebellion among the people. Because they saw themselves as grasshoppers, they acted like grasshoppers. They refused to believe God's promise and, consequently, they never entered the Promised Land.

Joshua and Caleb had also been part of the spy team and had seen the same giants. Unlike the other spies, however, they did not focus on the circumstances. Instead, they chose to believe God. They saw themselves as giants and acted like giants. As a result, they entered into the Promised Land and possessed it.

How often have you failed to possess the land—be it an opportunity, a ministry to which God has called you, health, or financial prosperity—because you focused on the giants—the problems and circumstances— instead of focusing on God's Word?

Decide today that no longer will you allow Satan to rob you of the blessings God wants to give you. Don't let the difficult situations in your life cloud your vision and thwart your success. Believe God and act as though you can do all things through Christ Who strengthens you. Act like a giant and you will be one.

Have you ever wondered why success follows some people while failure follows others? Is it a function of luck or heredity? Or is it the result of individual choice?

The reason that some succeed and some fail in life boils down to attitude. Basically, the difference between a grasshopper and a giant lies in their thinking.

A grasshopper is failure-conscious while a giant is success-conscious. A grasshopper riddles his vocabulary with "I can't's," while a giant saturates his with "I can's."

Let's look at some characteristic thought patterns of grasshoppers and giants. Where do you fit in?

GRASSHOPPERS	GIANTS
1. Let others control them.	1. Control themselves.
2. Are passive. Let life happen to them.	2. Are active. Make life happen.
3. See things as they are.	3. See things as they could be.
4. Settle for mediocrity.	4. Aspire to greatness.
5. Think "I can't."	5. Think "I can."
6. Look for excuses not to succeed.	6. Look for ways to succeed.
7. Are security-conscious.	7. Are willing to take risks.
8. Are past-oriented.	8. Are future-oriented.
9. Discourage others.	9. Encourage others.
10. Resist change.	10. Are open to change.

Did you find yourself in too many of the characteristics listed in column one? If so, take heart. All of us, at one time or another, have thought like grasshoppers.

The fact that you've read this far proves that you want to do something about your situation.

And because you want to, you can!

Chapter Two

Facts Don't Count!

Have you ever looked at the circumstances of your life and wanted to give up? I have. There have been times when I've felt, as Charles Swindoll puts it in his book by the same title, as though I were taking "three steps forward and two steps back." Until, that is, I learned what it means to walk by faith.

Walking by faith means choosing to believe God's Word instead of circumstances. The person who walks by faith knows that he must believe before he will see.

Our God is a God of faith. You may have just lost your home or been told that you have terminal cancer, but with God, FACTS DON'T COUNT! He doesn't see you as you see yourself. He sees you free and healed and saved.

Since God doesn't lie, it's extremely important that we learn what He says about us in His Word so that we can know who we are in Him. God is faithful to His Word. When He makes a promise, it doesn't matter what the circumstances look like. He will keep His promise if we simply trust Him to keep it. It is our faith not only in God's ability but also in His willingness to help us that makes the Word effective in our lives.

Abraham was 100 years old and Sarah 90 when their son Isaac was born. To the eyes of the world, the conception and birth of Isaac were a physical impossibility. But with God, all things are possible (Matthew 19: 26).

Are you facing a mountain in your life? Do you doubt your ability to overcome financial difficulties, to be healed of a serious illness, to rebuild a shattered marriage, to get out of the rut of mediocrity, to overcome a bad habit? Don't give up! Look up! Remember: facts don't count. Faith does!

Believing Is Seeing

What is faith? The Bible tells us that faith is "the confident assurance that something we want is going to happen. It is the certainty that what we hope for is waiting for us, even though we cannot see it up ahead" (Hebrews 11: 1 TLB).

Faith transcends facts, defies circumstances, and laughs in the face of setbacks. Faith chooses to believe the Word of God rather than the word of man. Faith makes you think and act like a giant.

As I was growing up, I often heard the expression "seeing is believing." You've probably heard the same expression and may even think it's true. But such thinking runs contrary to God's Word which says that believing is seeing

The world places final authority on the senses. The Christian, however, places final authority on the Word of God.

When we trust our senses above God's Word, we make a god of them. Moreover, trusting the senses more than God's Word contributes to poor self-esteem because our senses don't always tell us the truth about ourselves, whereas God's Word does.

Faith, on the other hand, looks beyond the senses into that spiritual realm which is more real than the physical one. Pat Robertson calls this spiritual realm "the secret kingdom" in his book by the same title.

A fundamental law in the secret kingdom is the law of faith. This law states that believing is seeing. When you understand the law of faith and master its operation, you take a major step forward toward discovering the greatness for which you were created. Why? Because faith is a force which produces an attitude. Faith in the negative, more commonly called fear, produces a negative attitude.

Your attitude, whether positive or negative, will reflect that in which you have faith.

Furthermore, you will draw to yourself the very thing in which you place your faith.

Take Job, for example. Most Christians think that Job had nothing to do with all the evils that came upon him. Yet he himself said, "What I always feared has happened to me" (Job 3: 25 TLB).

We will attract to ourselves that in which we place our faith. Before I learned about the law of faith and how it operates, I would catch the flu every year without fail. Because I believed that I would get the flu, it arrived right on schedule year after year. My faith was in sickness and sickness is what I got.

The same law of faith applies on the positive side. If you have faith in people, you will draw people to you. If you believe that you can succeed, you will attract success.

Fear and faith cannot exist in the same person at the same time. Make up your mind that you will always walk in faith. Develop an "I-can-do-it!" attitude and watch your fear disappear.

Faith vs. Fear

Basically, there are only two ways of looking at life: through the eyes of faith or the eyes of fear.

Fear is the perversion of faith. It has been said that fear is an acrostic for "false evidence appearing real." Too often we accept as true many situations that actually have no basis in reality. A child becomes frightened by a shadow on his bedroom wall and thinks it's a monster. A new, young executive is hired by a company and an older executive fears losing his job.

Like faith, fear is a spiritual force. While the force of fear itself is real, its methods are deceptive. Fear will cause you to believe the lies of Satan rather than the truth of God's Word. Fear will keep you from achieving greatness.

The Bible says that "God hath not given us the spirit of fear; but of power, and of love, and of a sound mind" (II Timothy 1: 7 KJV). As a believer in Jesus Christ, you have power over the force of fear. Begin using that power now to crush fear out of your life.

The Seed of Faith

"But how," you may be wondering, "do I get faith?" God tells us in His Word that He has given to every man "the measure of faith" (Romans 12: 3 KJV). This means that God, in His great mercy, has already planted the seed of faith in the heart of every person. It's up to us to water and nurture that seed so that it will grow.

How do we water and nurture the seed of faith? By listening to the Word of God and by doing it: "Yet faith comes from listening to this Good News—the Good News about Christ"

(Romans 10: 17 TLB). "And remember, it is a message to obey, not just to listen to" (James 1: 22 TLB).

As you listen to God's Word and obey it, faith will rise strong within you and fear will have to flee. That seed of faith which God planted in your heart will grow into a mighty oak and stand tall against the force of fear.

The Goliath Syndrome

The story of David and Goliath is a classic example of the power of faith to drive out fear. Here was a young boy, about seventeen years old, facing an arrogant, experienced, and ferocious warrior of enormous size and physical strength, and the only weapon David had was a slingshot.

From the looks of things, the confrontation was absurd. All common sense seemed thrown to the wind as the young David fearlessly approached his enemy.

Hearts beat fast as the two ill-matched opponents drew closer and closer to each other.

Goliath sneered impudently, confident of mastering the young boy.

With slingshot in hand, David moved steadily forward. Goliath moved likewise. But David did not see the towering giant before him. He refused to look at the circumstances. Instead, through the eyes of faith, David saw Goliath in the proper perspective as a mere man incapable of defeating the Almighty God.

David's thoughts were not thoughts of defeat but of victory. He shouted to Goliath, "You come to me with a sword and a spear, but I come to you in the Name of the Lord of the armies of heaven and of Israel—the very God Whom you have defied" (I Samuel 17: 45 TLB).

The rest of the encounter is history. Through the power of faith, David slew the mighty giant and won victory for the Israelites.

All of us at some point in our lives have suffered from "the Goliath Syndrome." We have allowed ourselves to be controlled by fear instead of faith. Like David's fellow Israelites, we have succumbed to spiritual paralysis by focusing on the problem instead of the solution.

Fear is a thief and a destroyer. Fear keeps you from launching out, from soaring like an eagle to unlimited heights of achievement and success.

You, the born-again believer in Jesus Christ, have the authority and the power to destroy fear in your life through His Name. Use that authority now and drive the spirit of fear from your life. Replace fear with faith.

Chapter Three

Psychological Escape-Hatches

We humans are a strange breed. We devise for ourselves all kinds of excuses for failing. Whenever we face a challenge, we leave ourselves options for retreat. I call these options "psychological escape-hatches."

A rampant and current example of a psychological escape-hatch is divorce. Many people marrying today do so with the mental reservation that if things get rough, they can always get a divorce. Never before in the history of mankind has divorce been viewed as a viable solution to marital problems to the extent that it is viewed today.

There are many other psychological escape-hatches which keep us from succeeding in life. Here are some of the most common:

The Age Excuse. "I'm too old (or too young) to try anything new." This psychological escape-hatch has kept countless persons from fulfilling God's dream for their lives.

Think of the people you know who have said things like "I'd really like to start my own business, but I'm too old," or "I've always wanted to take piano lessons, but it's too late." These people have allowed the illusive excuse of age to rob them of a fulfilling life.

I know a woman who began taking violin lessons at the age of thirty-three. By the time she was fifty-three, she was teaching violin and conducting orchestras as well.

I myself began taking cello lessons at the age of thirty-six. If I had used age as an excuse, I would have missed the wonderful experience of joining my husband and two young daughters in our own family string quartet.

No one really knows how many years are left to him. The twenty-year-old may have only five years left, while the sixty-year-old may have twenty. Age is merely a mental attitude. "You're as young as you think" is a psychological truism. Unfortunately, however, too many people allow the age excuse to shackle their dreams. As a result, they die with their song still imprisoned within them.

The Time Excuse. A wise man once said that all of us have enough time to do anything we really want to do. If our desire to do something is strong enough, we will find the time to do it.

God gives each of us 168 hours a week. How we use those hours determines how successful we become.

Life is like an hourglass. When the grains of time have dropped from top to bottom, they are gone forever. Perhaps time would be more precious to us if we had to check an internal hourglass instead of a wristwatch.

The average life span covers seventy years. One-third of those years you spend sleeping. Another third you spend at your job. That leaves you with only about twenty-three and one-third years to fulfill the dreams God has placed in your heart. Even this figure is high if you subtract time for grooming, traveling, and running errands.

You have, therefore, only about twenty years to fulfill your dreams. That's quite a sobering thought. Don't waste those few priceless years in aimless wandering. Seek God's goals for your life and make time to achieve them.

If you think you don't have time, you're right. But if you think you can make time, you're right too. Remember: you will act according to the way you think. The Bible says that as a man thinks in his heart, so is he (Proverbs 23: 7 KJV).

Part of your program of discovering your greatness is making the time to do those things that God has called you to do. When you persist with the time excuse, you chip away at your self-image. You begin secretly despising yourself for being so weak. Moreover, your life lacks enthusiasm because you are not answering the call of God's dream in you.

On the other hand, when you make the time to fulfill the desires God has placed within you, your self-esteem soars. You begin to feel good about yourself and about those around you.

Allowing yourself the time to accomplish God's dreams for your life gives you a sense of control over your life. You will be making things happen rather than letting them happen. You'll love yourself more and you'll be a happier person. In short, you'll be a giant.

The Intelligence Excuse. When I was growing up, great emphasis was placed on a person's IQ. I remember thinking that a high IQ automatically meant success.

Actually, IQ has little to do with success. There are thousands of people, brilliant by academic standards, who are failures in life. By the same token, there are thousands of others who, despite average IQ's, are among the most successful people in the world.

Intelligence has little to do with success. Attitude, however, has everything to do with it.

It has been said that your attitude, not your aptitude, determines your altitude. The next time you're tempted by the intelligence excuse, remember this saying.

The Health Excuse. Many people use poor health as an excuse for failure. They are unaware that God, in His great wisdom, has given the human body tremendous resiliency and recuperative powers. To flow in these powers through proper diet, rest, and exercise moves you toward success.

When poor health threatens your body, take measures to improve your physical condition. Exercise your faith in the Word of God and continue to work toward your goals. Refuse the temptation to quit. Press on. You will discover new strength welling up within you as you persevere physically in your journey toward success.

The Fear Excuse. This excuse manifests itself most commonly in three areas: the fear of people, the fear of failure, and the fear of success.

a) The fear of people. A good friend and business associate of mine once said, "Half the world is waiting for the other half to say 'hello.'" How sad but true! This fear of people often stems from childhood experiences of rejection or humiliation. If you struggle with this fear, realize that most other people have struggled with it too. You can overcome the fear of people by taking your eyes off yourself and concentrating on making others feel at ease.

The Bible has something to say about the fear of people: "For the Holy Spirit, God's gift, does not want you to be afraid of people, but to be wise and strong, and to love them and enjoy being with them" (II Timothy 1: 7 TLB).

People who are intimidated by other people have a poor self-image. They need you to reach out to them and to affirm them as worthwhile persons.

When you help others feel good about themselves, you become a more likable person, not only to them but to yourself as well. You take another step toward greatness

b) The fear of failure. An old proverb says that it is better to have tried and failed than never to have tried at all.

Most people take failure personally and regard it as a reflection of their self-worth. In reality, failure is simply a steppingstone to success.

The most outstanding success stories in history were fraught with failure.

Thomas Edison was probably the greatest inventor of all time. When nearly 10,000 experiments with a storage battery failed to produce positive results, a friend tried to console Edison.

"I have not failed," Edison replied. "I've just found 10,000 ways that won't work."

A failure is merely a detour in life, often leading you toward more beautiful and more productive paths. Like beauty, failure is in the eyes of the beholder.

The difference between a winner and a loser in life lies in their attitude toward failure. A loser stays down when he is knocked down. A winner gets up, brushes himself off, and tries again.

A loser looks on failure as defeat. A winner, however, looks on failure as a learning experience.

Learn from your failures and you'll be moving toward the greatness for which you were made.

c) The fear of success. The fear of success is surprisingly common. Symptoms of this fear are procrastination, laziness, and an inability to complete a task.

Deep inside, success-fearing people feel unworthy of success, so they don't bother trying.

Subconsciously, they look for excuses not to succeed.

As a Christian, you are worthy of success because Christ has made you so by His death and resurrection. God wants you to succeed. Your success brings Him glory and increases His impact in the earth.

Determine today that you are going to be successful for God. Commit your work to Him and watch it succeed.

The Money Excuse. Dr. Robert Schuller once said, "There is no such thing as a money problem; there are only idea problems."

Perhaps you've been thinking that your lack of money is keeping you from success. If so, consider Dr. Schuller's statement. Your problem is not a lack of money. It's a lack of money-generating ideas.

One of the curses from which Jesus redeemed us was the curse of poverty (II Corinthians 8: 9; Galatians 3: 13). As a Christian, you have been set free from financial bondage.

"But why," you may be asking, "do I still have more month at the end of my money?" Let me answer you with a question: "Do you tithe?"

The principle of tithing lies at the root of financial success. Many Christians can't make ends meet because they are not obeying God's command to tithe.

The Bible is replete with references to tithing. Proverbs 3: 9 TLB says, "Honor the Lord by giving Him the first part of all your income, and He will fill your barns with wheat and barley and overflow your wine vats with the finest wines."

Again, in Malachi 3: 10 TLB, God says, "Bring all the tithes into the storehouse so that there will be food enough in my Temple; if you do, I will open up the windows of heaven for you and pour out a blessing so great you won't have room enough to take it in!"

Giving God the first ten percent of your gross income provides Him with the seed necessary for Him to supply you with an abundant financial crop. According to God's Word, you will reap what you sow (Galatians 6: 7). If you plant financial seeds, you'll reap a financial harvest.

When you tithe, expect God to make good on His promise to you. Be open-minded. His response to your financial needs may be totally different from what you expect. He's an exciting, creative God with ideas you never dreamed possible. As you trust Him, He'll share some of these ideas with you and provide you with ways to become financially free. It's His desire that you "pay all your debts except the debt of love for others" (Romans 13: 8 TLB).

There is money out there to be earned. Ask God to show you how to earn it. In Proverbs 8: 12 TLB, God promises to give you "wisdom ... to discover knowledge and understanding" which you can use to create new ways of increasing your income.

As in all other areas of achieving greatness, the right attitude is crucial in the financial area too. Desiring money for the sake of money is not the right attitude. We all know that, to a certain degree, money is necessary to happiness. It's important to remember, however, that we must use money and love people, not love money and use people.

Finally, be a good steward of the money God has entrusted to your care. As you prove yourself trustworthy, He will increase His financial blessings in your life.

If you've been retreating from success through any of these psychological escape-hatches, decide now to close them tightly. Get rid of the excuses that keep you from discovering your greatness. Burn your bridges behind you and make a commitment today to fulfill God's dream for your life. You can do it!

Chapter Four

Shaping Your Circumstances

One of the greatest gifts God gave you is the freedom to choose. How you use this freedom will determine your failure or success in life.

No matter what your past has been—whether you're from Yale or jail—YOU can choose to make your future. YOU decide whether you will be a grasshopper or a giant in life.

Becoming a giant means being willing to change. It means being willing to give up negative habits and to replace them with positive ones. But the long-term rewards far outweigh the sacrifices. Indeed, as Zig Ziglar, well-known motivational speaker, often says, "You don't pay a price for success; you enjoy its benefits."

Begin today to enjoy the benefits of success by getting rid of negative habits that have caused you to fail. Decide to take charge of your life. Decide to be great.

The Buck Stops Here

Becoming great begins with accepting full responsibility for your actions. It's so easy to blame your parents, your environment, or your childhood circumstances for failure in your life. The truth is that YOU ALONE ARE RESPONSIBLE FOR YOUR ACTIONS.

For many people, this is a truth too painful to admit. It's much easier to find a scapegoat for failure. Acknowledging your total responsibility for your actions, however, frees you and puts you well on the road to discovering your greatness.

Mark was a young man of great potential and creativity. From all outward appearances, he had everything going for him.

Yet Mark was miserable and failing to become all that God created him to be.

Because of some tragic situations that had occurred during his childhood, Mark had allowed bitterness and resentment toward his parents to rob him of success. In his conversation, he repeatedly blamed his parents for his failure. He refused to face the fact that whether our past makes or breaks us is totally up to us.

It's not your past that matters; it's how you react to your past. Likewise, it's not your present situation that matters; it's how you respond to that situation. Facts don't count! Attitudes do!

Change: the Key to Growth

The word "change" strikes fear in the hearts of many people. Change forces us to move out of our comfort zone into unexplored, uncharted areas. But we don't like to move into the unknown simply because we don't know what's there. The familiar offers security and comfort.

Yet, you will never discover your greatness unless you are willing to change. Change implies growth. The opposite of change is stagnation.

Nothing in the universe ever remains static. It is moving either forward or backward. If you are not willing to change, you will not grow. If you do not grow, you will stagnate.

By refusing to change, you condemn yourself to a life of mediocrity and to a prison of psychological slavery. Resistance to change will keep you a grasshopper, while a willingness to change can make you a giant.

Your Will: the Key to Change

Although you may believe at present that you are a grasshopper, you can change that belief. You yourself hold in your hand the key to change. It's called your will. By an act of your will, you can decide right now that you are first-rate.

An amazing thing happens when you make such a decision. The message from your will travels down into your spirit and begins to take root there. You begin to see yourself as God sees you. You begin to realize that you are important and special. This, in turn, causes others to respond favorably to you, thus increasing your sense of self-esteem.

It's a cyclical process. When others love you, your self-esteem increases. But before you can love others, you must love yourself.

Jesus said, "Love your neighbor AS YOURSELF." This is such an important command that God mentions it in the Scriptures eight times (Leviticus 19: 18; Matthew 19: 19; 22: 39; Mark 12: 31; Luke 10: 27; Romans 13: 9; Galatians 5: 14; and James 2: 8).

For too long, Christians have overlooked the second part of Christ's injunction which, in reality, must come before the first part. Jesus is saying that you cannot love your neighbor unless you love yourself, for it is only out of a wholesome self-love that you can reach out to others in unconditional love.

"But," you may be asking, "how can I love myself when I feel like such a loser?" A close look at why you feel like a loser may help you to answer that question.

Causes of Poor Self-Esteem

Very few of us, if any, have escaped negative situations that have damaged our sense of self-worth. Perhaps the thoughtless comment of a parent or a teacher cut us to the quick. Or maybe a classmate or peer dealt a crushing blow to our self-image. Whatever the cause, all of us have suffered hurts that have left their scars on our psyches. These scars create obstacles to self-love.

Many people have poor self-images because they dwell on their past and refuse to believe that they can do anything about their future. They allow their past to condemn them to a life of mediocrity and failure.

Such people choose to live in an emotional and psychological stalemate because they believe man's word about them rather than God's Word. Seen in this light, the problem of poor self-esteem becomes, essentially, a problem of faith.

Often our feelings of poor self-esteem result from invalid comparisons. We compare our weakest points with the strongest points of others.

The problem arises from comparing in the first place. Second Corinthians 10: 12 AMP warns us that it's foolish to compare ourselves with one another: "... when they measure themselves with themselves and compare themselves with one another, they are without understanding and behave unwisely." Our goal must be to measure up to God's plan for us, not to measure up to others.

Your only competition should be with yourself. Remember that you are a unique creature, an original masterpiece straight from the Creator's hands. When God made you, He threw away the blueprint. Never has there been anyone just like you, nor will there ever be. Only you can do the work to which God has called you. You are important in God's plan.

"But I don't feel important," you protest. "So how can I honestly say I am important?" Good question. Here's the answer.

Faith: God's Measuring Rod

Feelings are not the yardstick in God's scheme of things. Faith is. The Bible says that "the just shall live by faith" (Romans 1: 17 KJV).

Faith believes what it does not yet see. Faith chooses to believe what God says about you in His Word, not what you feel about yourself.

God must be terribly grieved when His children refuse to believe what He says about them. Did you know that God calls us kings and priests, and even gods? Yes, even gods! (John 10: 34-35).

Will you dare to believe and act on what God says about you rather than on what others and you yourself say? If you do, you will be selling yourself on you.

Changing Your Self-Image

The level of your self-image determines the level of your success. As you begin to see yourself as God sees you, your level of self-esteem will rise. You will begin to accomplish things you never dreamed possible. But it's all up to you.

You CAN change your self-image from negative to positive. You CAN achieve any goal you conceive if you only believe.

"But," you may be thinking, "that's easier said than done. How can I erase years of negative programming overnight?"

Well, it probably won't happen overnight, but you can begin. And God's Word offers clear guidelines on how to do it through that wonderful transformation process called "the renewing of your mind" (Romans 12: 2 KJV).

Part II

The Transformed Mind

If you knew that you could not fail at anything you did, what would you do? Would you start that business you've been dreaming about since you were twenty? Would you take those art courses or earn that college degree? Undoubtedly, if you knew that you could not fail, you wouldn't hesitate to take that first step—and all subsequent steps—necessary to fulfill your dreams.

Yet, time after time, people allow the fear of failure to rob them of their dreams. Statistics show that only 20% of the human population realizes its dreams, while 80% settles for a life of mediocrity. Why? The answer lies in their thinking.

You are what you think about. Take a look at where you are in life right now. Are you doing what God has called you to do? Do you even know what God has called you to do? Are you growing? Are you becoming a better person? Are you drawing closer to Jesus? Or are you complacent, negative, and hopeless about your ability to make it?

Where you are right now in life is the direct result of what you've been thinking throughout your life. You are the sum and substance of your past thoughts.

Every action is the result of thought, whether conscious or subconscious. Thought is the seed which produces action. If you've been thinking negative thoughts, then your actions will be negative. If, on the other hand, you've been thinking positive thoughts, then your actions will be positive.

Chapter Five

Human Computers

When God created your mind, He engineered the most ingenious and intricate computer imaginable. In his book, *Success: the Glenn Bland Method* (Tyndale House, 1975, p. 9), Mr. Bland calls the mind "the last great 'unexplored' continent on earth." In this 48- ounce mass of marvelous brain tissue lies the key to your success or failure in life. God designed it this way. In creating you with a mind capable of free choice, He placed in your hands the key to your success.

Because your mind operates like a computer, it will not only absorb anything that is fed into it, but it will also give out precisely what has been fed into it.

Try this little experiment. Listen to yourself talk for the next ten minutes. You will probably be amazed at what you hear yourself saying.

Whatever comes out of your mouth was programmed into your mental computer by you or someone else during your lifetime. Most of us have had years of negative programming. Consequently, we do not see ourselves as successful nor as even possessing the ability to succeed. In many cases, we were programmed to believe that success is the result of luck or of being born with a silver spoon in one's mouth, to make matters worse, many of us were taught that success is sinful.

Yet God made us to succeed for His glory. Our failure does not glorify God. Our success does.

Keying in the Positive

But how do we get rid of negative thought patterns imbedded deep within our minds through years of wrong programming?

The answer lies in Jesus' command: "Be ye transformed by the renewing of your mind" (Romans 12: 2 KJV). With this command, Christ was giving us a key principle of success.

Jesus understood that we are what we think about. He understood that if we think we're failures, then we'll fail. If we think we're winners, then we'll win. In His own life, Jesus always thought positively. Never once did he entertain thoughts of failure or defeat.

Let's consider, for example, the time He was called to heal the daughter of Jairus, a ruler of the local synagogue (Luke 8: 41-56). While Jesus was accompanying the girl's father to their home, a messenger came to announce that the little girl had already died and that Jesus shouldn't bother coming. What did Jesus say? He said, "Don't be afraid; just believe, and she will be healed" (Luke 8: 50 NIV).

Jesus thought success and expected success. And success is what He always got.

Success begins with knowing who you are in Jesus Christ. When you made that life-changing decision to accept Christ as your personal Savior and Lord, you laid the only solid foundation for true success. As the Word says, He is the "Alpha and Omega" (Revelations 21: 6 KJV), the beginning and the end of all success. While the world offers its own formula for success, that formula ends ultimately in despair and eternal damnation.

Man was made for God. To seek success outside of God leads eventually to failure. The starting point of success, then, is to recognize your need for God.

Because of Adam and Eve's sin, every one of us is born into this world spiritually dead and separated from God. Only through Jesus Christ can we be reconciled to the Father. Jesus Himself said, "I am the Way, and the Truth, and the Life. No one comes to the Father except through Me" (John 14: 6 NIV).

When you accepted Jesus Christ as the mediator between you and the Father, your fellowship with God was instantly restored. You became a brand new person on the inside (II Corinthians 5: 17). You were born again.

Have you ever wondered, however, why after you were born again, you still had trouble overcoming certain bad habits? If so, I know how you feel, because I've faced the same struggle.

The reason for this dilemma is very simple. You are a triune being made up of a spirit, a soul (intellect, emotions, and will), and a body. Although you received a new spirit when you were born again, your mind and your body continued to operate according to the old you. Consequently, your old patterns of negative behavior continued to dominate you and will continue to do so unless you renew your mind through the Word of God.

While your spirit is positive, your mind and your body continually fight against your spirit (Romans 6). Christ calls you to renew your mind so that both your mind and your body can function in harmony with your spirit.

But what does it mean to renew your mind? Renewing your mind simply means replacing all the negative programming with the positive programming of God's Word. It means lining up your thinking with God's thinking. As you begin to do this, you will find yourself embarking on a new course of life which will be truly exciting and fulfilling.

Realistically, however, all the negative that has been programmed into your mind throughout your life will not disappear overnight. In fact, short of a miracle, it will never disappear because it is permanently etched into your memory. But don't let this fact discourage you. You can key so much positive into your mental computer that you will dilute the negative and render it virtually ineffective.

Verbal Print-Outs

Where should you begin? With the least suspected programmer in the world—your tongue. The Bible says that "death and life are in the power of the tongue" (Proverbs 18: 21 KJV). This tiny member of the body, as the Book of James so clearly points out, can create happiness or despair. It is a biblical fact—and principle as well—that we create our lives with our tongues.

Just as God spoke the universe into existence, so do we speak our own circumstances into existence (James 3).

The Bible is replete with verses on the power of the tongue. Through the words you speak, you program your mental computer either positively or negatively.

Picture your mind as a bank account. You can make deposits and you can make withdrawals, To a great extent, you control the deposits that are made into your mind. They can be either positive or negative. As for withdrawals, you have total control over them. You decide whether what comes out of your mind through your mouth will be positive or negative.

The way you speak determines the way you live. Most people do not realize the importance of the tongue in determining their future. WHAT YOU SAY IS WHAT YOU GET.

What do your verbal printouts sound like? Are they full of criticism, cynicism, and defeat? Or are they optimistic, positive, and enthusiastic?

Where you are in life now is the direct result of what you have been speaking. Moreover, what you have been speaking is the direct result of what you have been thinking, for out of the fullness of your heart, your mouth speaks (Matthew 12: 34). And what you have been thinking is the direct result of what you have been keying into your mental computer.

Doctors are discovering that many illnesses are not primarily the result of organic disorders but rather the result of wrong thinking and wrong speaking. Health—or sickness—begins on the inside and moves toward the outside.

You've probably heard comments like "My father died of a heart attack at age 59; I'll probably die the same way." Or, "Cancer runs in our family. I'm sure that's the way I'll go." Such thinking and speaking are dangerous. They are negative seeds planted in your mind which, if not uprooted, will produce a negative crop.

Right thinking and right speaking are essential to discovering your greatness. Determine today to think and speak only what God says about you in His Word. Anything else is a lie.

The following seven steps will help you to key in the positive:

1. DECIDE to eliminate negative patterns of thought and behavior. Negative patterns are any that do not line up with the Word of God.
2. DELIGHT in the Lord continually.
3. DIG into the Word daily and feed your spirit on God's wisdom.
4. DEVOTE yourself wholeheartedly to obeying the Word.
5. DEDICATE yourself totally to serving the Lord.
6. DECLARE continually what the Word says about you.
7. DETERMINE to press on despite setbacks.

Learning to key in the positive takes time, sometimes years. After all, it took years for you to be programmed negatively. At first, you may find yourself falling back into your old patterns of negative thinking and speaking. If you do, don't give up. As you persevere, you will find it progressively easier to be positive.

The Law of Genesis (or the Law of Compensation)

One of the fundamental laws of nature is the Law of Genesis, or the Law of Compensation. This law states that everything reproduces after its own kind (Genesis 1: 21, 25).

The Law of Genesis operates not only in the natural, physical realm, but in the mental and spiritual realms as well.

The Law of Genesis works like this. Suppose a farmer plants carrot seeds. What will he expect to harvest? Carrots, of course. To plant carrot seeds and expect peas would be ridiculous.

This same law applies in all other forms of reproduction: cats produce cats; people produce people.

The operation of the Law of Genesis is particularly significant in the mental, or thought, realm. When you plant positive thought seeds, you reap a crop of positive actions. When you plant negative thought seeds, you reap a crop of negative actions.

If you are down on yourself, it is the result of negative thought seeds that have been planted in your mind and are producing negative actions.

As children, we had very little control over what kinds of seeds were planted in our mental soil. Often, our present feelings of inferiority stem from the negative seeds planted by our parents, relatives, teachers, and peers.

There is a direct correlation between the kind of mental seed you plant and your self-image. When you plant positive thought seeds, the resulting positive actions build up your self-image. When you plant negative thought seeds, the resulting negative actions tear down your self-image.

Now think about this for a moment. When you plant a carrot seed, do you get only one carrot? Of course not. You get several carrots. Your seed is multiplied.

The same is true in the mental realm. When you plant a negative thought seed, it comes up multiplied many times over. The result is a harvest of negative worse than the original negative seed.

Zig Ziglar, in his best-selling book *See You At the Top* (Pelican, 1983, p. 226), explains it like this:

> The mind works like a garden…. Obviously you don't plant a bean to raise a bean—you plant a bean to raise lots of beans. Between planting and harvest there is a tremendous increase in the number of beans. That's the way the mind works. Whatever you plant in the mind is going to come up—multiplied. Plant a negative or a positive and you reap in multiples because between planting and harvest, imagination enters the picture and multiplies the result.

What are you reaping in your life right now? Health, prosperity, and peace of mind? Or strife, frustration, and financial lack? The harvest you are reaping right now indicates the kind of seeds you've been planting throughout your life.

In referring to the Law of Compensation in Galatians 6: 7-8 TLB, The Apostle Paul writes: "Don't be misled; remember that you can't ignore God and get away with it: a man will always reap just the kind of crop he sows. If he sows to please his own wrong desires, he will be planting seeds of evil and he will surely reap a harvest of spiritual decay and death; but if he plants the good things of the Spirit, he will reap the everlasting life which the Holy Spirit gives him."

If you've been planting negative seeds, repent and move on. There is a wonderful promise in the Book of Joel which says that God will restore to you the years that the locusts have eaten (Joel 2: 25 KJV). Claim this promise and trust God to fulfill it in your life.

Likewise remember: your mind is the soil, your tongue is the planter, and your words are the seeds. Check your conversation. Does it consist of a continuous string of negatives: "I can't make ends meet"; "I can't get anything done"; "I don't know what to do"; "I'm always so tired"?

Proverbs 6: 2 tells us that we are snared by the words of our mouths. If you say you can't, you're right. Likewise, if you say you can, you're right too. You will become what you think and speak about yourself.

The Bible warns us to keep watch over what goes into our minds and hearts (Proverbs 4: 23). What is in your heart will come out of your mouth and determine the circumstances of your life. If you want to discover your greatness, learn to control your tongue.

The As-If Principle

Have you ever had a bad toothache? If so, you know that you can't think of anything else but the throbbing pain.

Problems are like toothaches. They often cause so much pain that you can't think of anything but the problem. When you focus on the problem instead of the solution, however, you set the stage for fear and doubt to enter the picture. When fear and doubt come on the scene, faith leaves.

Becoming great means learning to focus on the solution instead of the problem. Romans 4: 17 TLB shows you how: "God ... speaks of future events with as much certainty as though they were already past." This verse reveals a spiritual law which I refer to as "the As-If Principle." Let's see how it works.

When you apply the As-If Principle, you simply act *as if* you already had the solution to your problem. In other words, you picture yourself free from that toothache.

Now this doesn't mean that you deny the problem. It simply means that you concentrate on its solution and seek ways to bring that solution about. Such concentration involves refocusing your vision from the negative to the positive. I will be the first to admit that sometimes this is very difficult to do. But the more you practice, the easier it becomes.

Have you ever noticed that most people constantly talk about their biggest problem, whether it be money, spouse, children, or health? By so doing, they reinforce its stronghold in their lives.

Verbal repetition of the problem strengthens its image in your mind and etches that image more deeply into your subconscious. If you dwell on the negative image long enough, it will eventually become a reality in your life.

The opposite is true as well. Verbal repetition of what God's Word says about your problem creates faith in your heart for its solution. Romans 10: 17 NIV tells us that "faith comes from hearing the message, and the message is heard through the word of Christ."

This faith, in turn, will cause God to move on your behalf because without faith it is impossible to please Him (Hebrews 11: 6). When God moves on your behalf, the solution to your problem becomes manifest in your life.

Let's look at an example. God applied the As-If Principle when He told Abraham and Sarah that they were going to have a son. God changed Abram's name to "Abraham," which means "Father of Many Nations." He also changed Sarai's name to

"Sarah," which means "Princess." Furthermore, God foretold that she would be the mother of nations (Genesis 17: 16).

Now why did God change their names? For a very important reason. As Sarah called Abraham in for dinner every night, she was now calling him "Father of Many Nations." Her verbal repetition of Abraham's new name created in his mind an image of himself as, indeed, the father of many nations. Hearing the word "Abraham" again and again increased his faith.

When Abraham was 100 years old and Sarah was 90, their son Isaac was born. Abraham and Sarah saw their promised child because even before he was born, they had spoken of those things which were not as though they were.

An incident from my own life illustrates another application of the As-If Principle. One of our daughters had developed the negative habit of chronic complaining. It was becoming so bad that I found myself continually reprimanding her. One day, while my husband and I were analyzing the situation, it suddenly occurred to me that I had been reinforcing our daughter's negative behavior by repeatedly drawing her attention to it. I had created in her a mental image of herself as a complainer, and she had lived up to that image.

I immediately changed my tactics. I began introducing her as "my daughter with the positive attitude." Within a matter of days, she had made an almost complete turn-about. Because I was reinforcing the positive, she became positive. Today, with only an occasional slip, she maintains a healthful, positive attitude and is a delight to have around.

When you apply the As-If Principle to your life, the positive mental images you create will generate verbal printouts that are geared to success. You can use this principle in whatever situation you find yourself. Speak those things that are not as though they were. Then, believe what you speak and it will be.

Chapter Six

Your Attitude Control Center

NASA with all its sophisticated machinery could never match the magnificent equipment God has placed inside your head. Unfortunately, most people never learn how to use that equipment properly. Knowing how to do so—and doing so—will literally change your life. I'm talking about your attitude control center. Did you know that you alone have total control over your attitude? No other person or circumstance can affect how you think without your permission.

What exactly is attitude?

Attitude is a particular way of looking at a situation. Webster defines attitude as "a mental position with regard to a fact or state."

Your attitude may be positive or negative. Which one it will be is totally up to you.

Your Attitude is Showing

Your attitude affects everyone around you. If you're cheerful and optimistic, you create a positive response in others. If you're negative and gloomy, people don't want to be around you. Wherever you are and whatever you do, your attitude is showing.

Contrary to popular belief, you can learn to have a positive attitude. While it is true that some temperaments have a greater struggle than others in cultivating and maintaining a positive outlook on life, such an attitude can be acquired by anyone who is willing to learn.

A positive attitude attracts people. It gives you a magnetic personality. It helps you to discover your greatness.

But how do you develop a positive attitude?

Developing a Positive Mental Attitude

Developing a positive mental attitude begins with you. Many people believe that a good attitude depends on external circumstances. These people make comments like, "When I get a good job, everything will be all right," or "When I get married, then I'll be happy." Such thinking is deceptive and leads only to unhappiness and failure.

When we allow external circumstances—like the weather, the stock market, or the news—to determine our attitude, we are nothing more than slaves to fickle taskmasters. Achieving greatness requires assuming total responsibility for your attitude despite external circumstances. When you assume total responsibility for your attitude, you can always be positive no matter what happens. You take control of your life instead of letting it take control of you.

Attitude is a learned habit. If you're negative, you learned how to be negative. If you're positive, you learned how to be positive. Since attitude is a habit, you can change a bad attitude into a good one simply by developing a new habit.

Psychologists tell us that it takes an average of twenty-one days to develop a habit. If you've ever moved to a new home, you may recall that it took you about three weeks to adjust to your new surroundings. The same is true of a new job or a new school.

Likewise, when developing a new habit, you will need about twenty-one days before the habit becomes second-nature to you.

If you've been negative all of your life, take heart. You can become a radiant, positive, magnetic person. All it takes is desire, a decision, and action.

And let me tell you a wonderful secret. You will discover, in the process of achieving greatness, that your greatest weakness is simply the obverse of your greatest strength. If you have been a critical person, you can become a great encourager. If you have been callous, you can become gentle and kind.

You alone can decide to develop a positive mental attitude. Here are two keys that will help you to unlock the doors of positive thinking:

1. MEDITATE ON GOD'S WORD EVERY DAY. The Bible tells us that God's words are "spirit, and they are life" (John 6: 63 KJV). When you meditate on God's Word—that is, think about it and put it into practice in your life—you are tapping into the very source of life itself and energizing your mind with positive charges.

2. KEEP CAREFUL WATCH OVER WHAT GOES INTO YOUR MIND THROUGH YOUR EARS AND YOUR EYES. What you allow to enter your mind eventually comes out of your mouth in the words you speak. And what you speak will come to pass. Proverbs 4: 23 NIV admonishes us in this regard: "Above all else, guard your heart, for it is the wellspring of life." Do you want a polluted wellspring, filled with negative thoughts? Or do you want a wellspring filled with the sweet-tasting water of positive thinking? The choice is up to you.

Chapter Seven

Harnessing Your Thought Power

A raging river carries within itself the potential to supply tremendous energy to turn the wheels of industry. Unless that river is harnessed, however, its energy is aimlessly diffused, with no resultant productivity.

Your mind, like that river, also flows with abundant energy in the form of thoughts. But unless those thoughts are harnessed, their potential power will be dissipated, resulting in a life of idleness and discontent.

Harnessing your thought power simply means channeling it toward positive ends. It means taking those thoughts that are constructive and using them to build goals and to fulfill dreams.

Philippians 4: 8 TLB provides the foundational principle for harnessing your thought power: "Fix your thoughts on what is true and good and right. Think about things that are pure and lovely, and dwell on the fine, good things in others. Think about all you can praise God for and be glad about."

Casting Down Imaginations

In II Corinthians 10: 5 we learn that any thought that enters your mind has the potential of passing through the following three stages: the thought stage, the imagination stage, and the stronghold stage. When a thought enters your mind, it is initially only a thought. You can dismiss it or choose to entertain it.

If you choose to entertain the thought, it then becomes an imagination. This means that you begin to visualize it in your mind's eye. It takes on a more definite shape and assumes a greater control over you.

For example, let's suppose that it's almost lunchtime. You are beginning to feel hungry and the thought of apple pie and ice cream enters your mind. Because you're hungry, you begin to entertain that thought. You begin to visualize the warm pie, chock full of apples and smothered with a huge dip of vanilla ice cream. Your mouth begins to water, and you can almost taste that pie, the image is so clear. At this point, your thought has become an imagination.

If you continue to dwell on the imagination, it then moves into the realm of a stronghold. That is, it becomes an obsession from which you find it virtually impossible to retreat. You will feel that you must have that apple pie. It will take on an insistent, obsessive nature, and before you know it, you'll be eating apple pie and ice cream for lunch.

The thought of apple pie and ice cream is in itself rather benign, unless you are a glutton. Other thoughts, however, are not so harmless. Take, for example, the thought of adultery. It too begins only as a thought. If not dismissed, it becomes an imagination and finally a stronghold which brings nothing but death and destruction in its wake.

The Bible clearly warns us to cast down imaginations and to bring every thought under the rulership of Jesus Christ (II Corinthians 10: 5). Strongholds will draw you away from Christ and lead you to destruction. For this reason, it is so important to guard your ears and your eyes from anything that could cause a negative or sinful thought to enter your mind. If you nip the negative thought in the bud, its chances of developing into an imagination and a stronghold are eliminated.

Why is it so important to control your thoughts? It's important because thought produces action. As in the case of the apple pie, you will act on what you think about most. If you think negative thoughts, then your actions will be negative. Conversely, if you think positive thoughts, then your actions will be positive.

Remember: ACTION IS THE FRUIT OF THOUGHT.

Putting On the Mind of Christ

Harnessing your thought power involves putting off the carnal mind and putting on the mind of Christ.

What is the carnal mind? The carnal mind is the mind that is controlled by the senses rather than by the Word of God. The carnally-minded person allows his fleshly desires to dominate him. He surrenders to quarreling, jealousy, anger, slander, gossip, arrogance, pride, and sexual impurity (II Corinthians 12: 20-21).

While these characteristics of carnal thinking are more readily observable, there is another side to carnal thinking that is often overlooked by Christians. Carnal thinking is any thinking that does not line up with the Word of God. For example, your checkbook shows that you do not have enough money to pay the rent. The Word of God, on the other hand, tells you that if you have faithfully tithed your income, God will supply all your needs.

You now have a choice. You can believe what your checkbook shows, or you can believe what the Word of God says. To believe your checkbook is to act according to what your senses tell you. It is to be carnally-minded, or sense-minded. To believe the Word of God, on the other hand, is to act according to what your spirit tells you. It is to be spiritually-minded.

Of course, you must accompany your faith in God's Word with action, for faith without works is dead (James 2: 17). God will not usually drop a large sum of money into your lap so that you can pay your bills. Normally, He provides through natural channels of effort on your part.

The Bible says that to be carnally-minded is death, but to be spiritually-minded is life (Romans 8: 6). Far too many Christians have not developed their potential in Christ because they have lived most of their Christian lives thinking carnally. They have responded to situations according to what their senses told them instead of what God's Word says.

For example, in the area of finances, they have said, "I'm broke"; "I can't pay my bills"; "I don't know how we're going to make it." In the area of health, they have said, "My asthma is getting worse;" "My eyes are going bad;" and a host of other negatives which block the flow of God's blessings in their lives.

It is not God Who withholds blessings from His children. It is His children who, through unbelief, create obstacles to receiving His blessings. Instead of believing what God says about them, they believe the lies of Satan. They allow those lies to become strongholds in their lives. Consequently, those lies spawn sickness, poverty, strife, and every evil thing.

You do not have to be sick. You do not have to be poor. You do not have to be a failure. You do not have to feel inferior. But as long as you accept as true those things that are really lies, you will never discover your greatness, for you will receive that in which you place your faith.

Any thought that comes to your mind and that does not line up with the Word of God is a lie. This is the reason it is so important for you to be saturated with the Word of God. Immerse yourself in it. Meditate on it day and night so that you will know what is the truth and what is a lie. Health and prosperity are truth. Sickness and poverty are lies.

The very instant a thought enters your mind, you can choose to accept it or reject it. You are the doorkeeper of your mind. You choose what will enter into it. God says, "I have set before you life and death, blessing and cursing: therefore choose life, that both thou and thy seed may live" (Deuteronomy 30: 19 KJV).

How do you choose life? There are two steps:

1) Refuse to receive into your mind any thought that does not line up with the Word of God.

2) Offer your body (your senses) as a living sacrifice to God (Romans 12: 1).

This means surrendering your senses to God so that His Word can control them. Then, and only then, will they lose their power to deceive you.

Decide today to harness your thought power and to submit it to the Lordship of Jesus Christ. Begin to think as He thinks.

Since Christ and His Word are one, then putting on the mind of Christ simply means thinking in agreement with His Word. As you do, you will be one step closer to becoming great.

Chapter Eight

The Single Eye

Have you ever taken your eye off the road for a split second while driving and nearly had an accident? You soon learned that safety tolerates no distractions. You must keep your eyes focused on the road ahead to avoid a collision.

The same is true in the process of renewing your mind. The transformed mind is a single mind, a mind that looks straight ahead. It is a mind that does not vacillate but can make a decision and stick to it. It is a mind that knows where it's going and how to get there.

I struggle with a tendency to get sidetracked. I begin a task in one room and then walk into another room, only to forget the earlier task and begin a new one. This is a weakness which I am slowly overcoming, thanks to God's grace working in me.

Allowing yourself to be sidetracked is a sure way to keep yourself from becoming great. When you get sidetracked, you rarely accomplish what you set out to do because you take your eyes off your goal. Consequently, you don't feel good about yourself.

The sidetracked person's life consists of bits and pieces of partially completed projects. He rarely, if ever, savors the joy of achieving a predetermined goal.

If you've ever taken a trip, you know that you must first decide on a destination. Then you must keep your eye on that destination no matter what detours you may encounter along the way. This singleness of purpose—or the single eye—is a key factor in achieving greatness in life.

But there are forces at work to keep you from having a single eye and, consequently, from fulfilling your dreams. These forces may be grouped under the heading of "double-mindedness." They have kept many Christians from realizing their potential in Christ. Let's examine the most common of these forces and learn how to overcome them.

The Dangers of Double-Mindedness

Double-mindedness, as the term indicates, is the state of having two minds, or of going mentally in two directions at the same time. The Bible says that the double-minded person should not expect to receive anything from the Lord (James 1: 7).

The double-minded person lacks confidence. He fears making a mistake and, as a result, remains in a stalemate. He fails to realize, however, that not to make a decision is in itself a decision.

Because of its inherent division, double-mindedness leads to those weaknesses that result from a split mind: worry, indecision, procrastination, and depression. All of these are tools of Satan to rob you of your effectiveness for Christ and of the blessings He has for you. Let's take a look at these weaknesses.

Worry

Worry is simply dwelling on negative thoughts instead of positive ones. Worry is a sin and results only in destruction.

Many Christians find it extremely difficult to keep from worrying. If you are a worrier, you can overcome this dangerous habit. Just remember this: the thought process you use to worry is exactly the same thought process you use not to worry.

Worrying involves your imagination. When you worry, you allow your mind to dwell on negative images. These negative images arouse fear which only creates more negative images. It is a vicious cycle. But you can stop it.

Like other struggles you face, worrying is a habit. Here are some practical steps to help you overcome the worry habit:

1. Realize that, as statistics have shown over and over again, most of what you worry about never happens.

2. Every time a worry thought assails you, replace it with a positive thought.

3. Spend five minutes a day imagining the opposite of what you've been worrying about.

4. Admit that worrying is a sin. Repent and stand on the Scripture promise that you have a sound mind (II Timothy 1: 7). A worrying mind is not sound.

5. Recognize that worry is a spiritual force. Deal with it spiritually by using the Word of God against it. This means that whenever you are tempted to worry, obey God's command to cast your cares on Him (I Peter 5: 7).

6. Learn to keep your eyes on Jesus. The Word says, "Thou wilt keep him in perfect peace, whose mind is stayed on thee: because he trusteth in thee" (Isaiah 26: 3 KJV). Trust comes from knowing a person. When you read God's Word, you get to know Him better, and you come to realize that He is perfectly faithful, dependable, and trustworthy. He will never let you down.

7. Get your eyes off yourself and reach out to other people. Put a smile on your face and begin to enjoy life, knowing that God loves you and will take care of you.

Worry is one of the biggest killers today. It can lead to heart disease and all kinds of physical and mental disorders. Worry will keep you from becoming great.

Procrastination

"I'll start my diet tomorrow." How often have you heard that momentous statement or perhaps even said it yourself? I too must confess that those words have crossed my lips more than once.

Human creatures that we are, we readily find excuses for postponing those things we ought to do. But putting off what you know you should do—or procrastinating—is a sure way of robbing yourself of self-esteem.

What causes people to procrastinate? There are several reasons:

1. LAZINESS. Not much is said today about laziness, yet the Bible mentions it several times. Proverbs 6: 9 NIV de-

scribes the devastating effects of laziness: "How long will you lie there, you sluggard? When will you get up from your sleep? A little sleep, a little slumber, a little folding of the hands to rest— and poverty will come on you like a bandit and scarcity like an armed man." Laziness is a thief. It will cause you to miss out on God's will for your life. It will keep you from doing what you should do to reach your goals.

2. LACK OF DISCIPLINE. It takes discipline to maintain a single eye. People who lack discipline find excuses to keep from doing what they know they should be doing. The undisciplined person falls into the same category as the lazy person who allows circumstances to control him rather than controlling circumstances.

3. LACK OF DIRECTION. Goals are essential to a well-ordered life. Without goals, you merely sail from one day to the next, floundering aimlessly with no purpose in life. In a later chapter, we shall discuss in detail how to set goals and achieve them.

4. THE FEAR OF SUCCESS. Perhaps more than any of the above, the root cause of procrastination is the fear of success. "Why would anyone fear success?" you make ask. I asked the same question several years ago. Many people, especially Christians, fear success because of a deep sense of guilt that attaches to it. False teaching has caused many Christians to look on themselves as worthless. Many of the lyrics of the hymns we sing in church promote this image. How, then, can we justify success for worthless creatures?

And so we plod along, without goals or purpose, until that tragic day when we look back and ask ourselves what might have been.

Don't fall into the procrastination trap. Avoid it at all costs, for it is indeed a mental plague that will keep you from greatness.

Indecision

Do you remember the children's game "Eeny-Meeny-Miny-Mo?" As a child, I often used this game when facing a decision. When I had my own children, I watched them and their friends do the same thing. It is much easier to allow chance to decide for you than to take the bull by the horns and make the decision yourself.

Indecision is double-mindedness in its most elemental form. It is a dangerous crippler that will keep you from moving ahead toward your goals. Moreover, the very act of not deciding is in itself a decision.

If you suffer from indecision, here are some suggestions that will help you to overcome it:

1. When faced with a decision, pray. Ask God to guide you into His perfect will for your life.

2. Take a sheet of paper and divide it into two columns. Label one column "Advantages" and the other "Disadvantages."

3. List all the advantages and disadvantages of a particular decision. If the advantages outweigh the disadvantages, and if you can live with the consequences of your decision, then go ahead with it.

4. Take action. Do something right away that will implement your decision.

5. Refuse to look back. As Paul says, "forgetting those things which are behind ... press toward the mark" (Philippians 3: 13-14 KJV).

Depression

In his fine book, *Self-Love* (The Berkley Publishing Group, 1978, pp. 87-88), Dr. Robert Schuller discusses the role of creativity in building self-worth. Since we were created to think and act, any long-term interference with the proper functioning of our thinking and acting abilities weakens our self-esteem.

The double-minded person is a prime target for depression because his thinking and acting abilities are not functioning properly. He is caught between two conflicting paths and is unable to choose one. Consequently, he feels weak and ineffective and beyond the hope of cure.

Satan loves to attack Christians through depression. It is a very effective tool against the furthering of the kingdom of God. Depression causes you to feel unworthy, to lose the confidence that is in you. But the Word says that we should "lay hold upon the hope set before us" (Hebrews 6: 18 KJV). That hope, if nurtured, will eventually ignite faith that, in turn, will dispel depression.

We serve a big God. His Word says that you can do all things through Christ who strengthens you—all things, not some (Philippians 4: 13). You can shake off the grip of depression through the Name of Jesus. Believe that you are important. Keep your eye on the Word of God. Refuse to give in to negative thoughts about yourself. Picture yourself as happy, successful, and a blessing to others.

Finally, look around you. There are many hurting people who need the words of comfort and hope that only you can give. By reaching out to others, you will be doing much toward becoming great.

The Established Heart

There's a lot of talk these days about burnout. We live in such a fast-paced society that it doesn't take much to feel literally "burned-out" from the pressures of life. A few hours of driving on nearly any turnpike will attest to this fact.

But God's way doesn't lead to burnout. He wants you to experience His peace even in the midst of the greatest pressure. The Scripture passage about the storm at sea clearly illustrates this truth (Matthew 8: 23-27).

The Apostles' boat was being rocked by violent winds while Jesus slept peacefully in the back of the boat. How many of us could sleep in the midst of hurricane-force winds? Yet this is precisely the kind of peace God wants for us and has provided for us.

Peace in the midst of every storm is not merely a nice phrase but a powerful reality. But how can we experience this peace when problems and pressures relentlessly bombard us at every turn?

Psalm 112: 7-8 tells us that if our hearts are fixed on God, we shall not be afraid of bad news because our trust is in the Lord, not in man. By keeping your mind focused on Jesus, you will experience perfect peace. This is what it means to have an established heart.

When our younger daughter was seven years old, she broke her arm. I was about 200 miles from home when I received word of her injury. As I covered the highway miles on my way home, I felt the peace of Christ flood my soul. I wanted desperately to be with my little girl, but Jesus assured me that all was well and that He was watching over her. Because my heart was established in Him, I had perfect peace in the midst of the storm.

What a great blessing it is to know that Jesus is always by your side! He promised never to leave you nor forsake you (Hebrews 13: 5).

Determine today that you will establish your heart in God. Here are two proven principles that will help you:

1. Let God's Word dominate your thoughts. Psychologists tell us that we gravitate toward our most dominant thought. If your most dominant thought is Jesus, then you will automatically gravitate toward Him in every situation. Your immediate response to any situation, good or bad, will be based on God's Word hidden within you. Because of this, you will walk in perfect peace.

2. Memorize passages of the Word that are especially meaningful to you. When the Word is hidden in your

heart, it will grow and provide strength in your time of need.

Establish your heart in God and get rid of fear. When you do, you can't help but be a winner!

Part III

Learning to Love Yourself

When was the last time you looked at yourself in the mirror and said "I love you"? If you haven't done so lately, you should.

Loving yourself is a biblical commandment. In Romans 13: 9 NIV Paul writes, "You shall love your neighbor as *yourself*" (Italics mine). This means that you are to love your neighbor in the same manner and to the same degree that you love yourself. But if you don't love yourself, you can't love your neighbor. Loving others begins with loving yourself.

Satan has deceived generations of Christians into believing that self-love is egotism. Egotism, however, is directly opposed to self-love. Unlike self-love, egotism is pure selfishness. In his excellent book, *The Art of Loving* (Perennial Library, Harper & Row, 1974, p. 51), Erich Fromm writes that "selfishness and self-love, far from being identical, are actually opposites."

Why do we feel so uneasy about loving ourselves? Christians, especially, have difficulty in this area because of erroneous teaching on humility which has traditionally prevailed in the Church. For far too long, Christians have been taught that humility means putting yourself down. To be humble does not mean that at all. On the contrary, true humility means recognizing the authority, worth, dignity, and power you have in Christ. If God thought you important enough to die for you, then you have no right to consider yourself a worm.

A humble person is not a mouse. He is a lion. He recognizes that he is special because of God living in him. When we put ourselves down, we deny the living God who indwells us. How we must grieve the Holy Spirit when we project a false image of weakness and defeat.

In fact, putting yourself down is a kind of hypocrisy in reverse. A hypocrite is one who projects an external image that conflicts with what he really is on the inside. He pretends to be something he is not. But what about Christians whose outward demeanor of inferiority contradicts who they really are on the inside—new creatures in Christ?

Loving yourself as God loves you is true humility. This means seeing yourself as God sees you. God sees you as a mighty warrior capable of defeating every onslaught of the enemy through the blood of Christ. You are not a grasshopper. You are a giant!

Self-love becomes egotism when it looks on itself as the source and the end. Biblical self-love, however, recognizes that you are made in the image of God and that, for this reason alone, you are special. As Dave Grant points out in his superb book on love, *The Ultimate Power* (Fleming H. Revell, 1983, p. 19), "Our self-worth is a given. What we've been working so hard to get, we've already got! A self worth loving!"

The world has set up many false standards for human worth. At one time or another, we have all fallen prey to those standards. The chief among them are looks, intelligence, and performance. These have become the false gods of our age. We are loved not for who we are but for what we do, how we look, and how we perform.

When meeting a new person, haven't you often asked or been asked the question, "What do you do?" It's almost expected. And how often have we judged or been judged by our occupation? If we are honest with ourselves and with one another, we will admit that a person who says he is a physician carries more esteem in our eyes than one who says he is a trash collector. Yet each one is just as important in God's sight as the other.

Denis Waitley, world-renowned behavioral psychologist, tells of an experiment he often does with children. Taking a group of volunteers, he asks each child to assume the role of a person in a predetermined occupation. One child takes the role of a doctor, another a plumber, another a homemaker, and so on. Then Dr. Waitley directs the children to line themselves up in order of importance. Invariably the child playing the doctor places himself at or near the head of the line, while the child playing the trash collector automatically assumes the position at the end of the line.

This is a sad commentary on the value system of our culture. At a very early age, children have already absorbed the lies of our false societal gods.

The same is true of looks and intelligence. We tend to label people as important or unimportant based on how they look or how much they know. A person with a string of titles after his name is considered of greater worth to society because of what he knows than a high school dropout who supposedly has much less to contribute.

This dangerous attitude of expediency has its roots in the philosophy of humanism which determines human worth by a person's usefulness to society. Only those who can perform—and perform well—are of any value. This eliminates the handicapped, the retarded, and the elderly. The increase in infanticide and euthanasia in this country attests to this humanistic way of thinking.

Dave Grant notes the results of this false societal standard of performance:

> The standard that says our self-worth is determined by what we do is the most deadly because efficiency becomes society's number one value. And unless society is knit together with love there is only efficient organization; and when efficiency is the highest value, persons are transformed into things whose value is their contribution to making things run. Without love, efficiency can excuse everything; the weak, the voiceless, the unborn may all be sacrificed at the altar of efficiency (Ibid., p. 38).

An attitude of expediency results from comparing one person to another. But the Bible clearly states that comparing is not wise (II Corinthians 10: 12). When we compare, we measure our worth in terms of another human being instead of God's terms. Comparing is a dangerous practice. There will always be people who can do certain things better than you can and those who cannot. But this has nothing to do with their worth as persons.

Only genuine love—God's kind of unconditional love—can overcome an attitude of expediency. And loving with God's kind of love begins with loving yourself as God loves you. God's love for you is not based on your looks, your intelligence, or your performance. He loves you because you are you. And you too must love yourself in the same way.

Dr. Schuller writes: "It's not a sin to experience a wonderful feeling of self-affection. It is a sin not to love what God loves" (ibid., p. 12). Refusing to love yourself is a slap in the face of God. It is telling Him that He made a mistake when He made you.

Our lack of self-love, however, is usually not deliberate because deep down, all of us want to love ourselves. We simply don't know how. The road to self-love can be a painful and rocky one. Let's look at some ways that will help you to make the journey a little smoother.

Chapter Nine

Accepting Yourself

Have you ever wished you were someone else? Most of us have at some point in our lives. Or have you ever complained, "If only my skin were a different color, then I'd make it," or "If only I had Jim's brains, I'd land that job"?

Most people are dissatisfied with themselves in some way. In a survey of women made several years ago, more than 70% of the respondents stated that they were dissatisfied with their physical appearance. I would venture to say that many men would respond the same way.

There are things about yourself that you can change and things that you cannot change. Accepting yourself involves, first of all, the ability to distinguish between the two. Furthermore, it involves changing those things that you can change and accepting those things that you cannot change.

If you never grew beyond four-foot-ten, there's no use lamenting that you're not six-four. You would do better expending your energy elsewhere. Moreover, it's not the size of the man in the fight that counts; it's the size of the fight in the man.

When you accept yourself, you see yourself through God's eyes. You acknowledge His wisdom in creating you. This alone is sufficient to give your life dignity and meaning. Your inherent worth as a human being derives not from what you do but from who you are in the sight of God.

When you accept yourself, you squarely face your strengths and weaknesses. You choose to capitalize on your strengths and to overcome your weaknesses.

A word of caution here: self-acceptance is not complacency. While you accept those things that you cannot change, you recognize, nevertheless, the necessity for continued growth and development in every area of your life. You are always seeking to better yourself for the glory of God.

Here are some proven steps to help you accept yourself:

1) Set aside a few moments to make a list of your strengths and weaknesses. Divide a sheet of paper into two columns with the headings "My Strengths" and "My Weaknesses."

    Next to each weakness, write down one thing you will do today to overcome that weakness. If, for example, you eat too much, write down something you will do to change this bad habit. Use a positive sentence to state your action instead of a negative one. For example, instead of writing "I will not eat dessert," write, "I eat only low-fat foods." When you concentrate on the positive, you program your mind to look favorably on the process of overcoming your weaknesses. Moreover, positive affirmations have a way of implanting themselves more readily into your subconscious mind.

    When you have finished your list of strengths and weaknesses, make another list of those things about yourself that you can change and those things that you cannot change (for example, your ancestry, your height, the color of your eyes and skin). Beside each item that you can change, list something you will do today to change it. Beside each item that you cannot change, write "I accept this feature about myself. I trust God's wisdom in creating me this way, a special, unique person, unlike any other."

2) Be patient with yourself. Realize that you are a masterpiece in the making. As Bill Gothard says in his national seminars, "God is not finished with you yet.

    Compliment yourself when you do something right. When you miss the mark, say, "That wasn't like me. I'll do better next time."

When you accept yourself, you are pursuing greatness. When you don't accept yourself, you become your own worst enemy. Often, conflicts between people result because of a lack of self-acceptance. When you are down on yourself, you project your feelings of inferiority onto others. You become resentful and bitter when all the while the problem lies with you.

Self-acceptance and self-image are intimately linked. When your self-image is good, you will accept yourself. On the other hand, when your self-image is poor, you will have difficulty accepting yourself.

What is self-image and how can you change it? Your self-image is the mental picture of yourself that you carry around with you. It is the composite of beliefs that you have held about yourself throughout your life. These beliefs have come from your past experiences—your successes, your failures, the remarks and actions of others toward you.

As children, we believe everything that our parents and teachers tell us. Unfortunately, however, although some of their comments about us were false, our minds accepted them as true. Consequently, if your father called you "stupid," then, most likely, you believed that you were stupid.

All of your past experiences are pieces in the puzzle of your self-image. But for most people, the pieces of that puzzle were constructed from lies.

In writing about self-image in his best-selling book, *Psycho-Cybernetics* (Pocket Books, 1960, p. 2), Dr. Maxwell Maltz states: "All your actions, feelings, behavior—even your abilities—are always consistent with this self-image." In other words, how you see yourself will always determine how you will act.

For example, if you see yourself as a total failure, you will act like one. No matter how hard you try to do otherwise, you will always find ways to fail. In short, you will act according to your self-image.

This means that you will never achieve in life beyond the level of your self-image. If you are like most people, your self-image is not where it should be. But I have good news for you. You can change your self-image. Here's how:

- Decide that you want to change your self-image. If you don't want to, you won't. Remember that desire is the starting point of all achievement.

- Understand that your self-image is the result of all of your life experiences and that, in most cases, the input from these experiences was false. For instance, you may have gotten D's all through school and been labeled a slow learner. Because society has said that D students usually don't succeed, you see yourself as a failure.

- But what does a D say about your self-worth? Absolutely nothing. Your self-worth is not dependent on what grades you earned in school. It is given to you by God simply because He created you. There's not a thing you can do or need to do to earn your self-worth.

- Indicate by your actions that you value yourself. Here are some suggestions:

- When you make a phone call, give your name immediately after the greeting. For example, say, "Good morning, this is Martha Howard. I would like to speak with Mr. Simpkins." Also, when you answer the phone, give your name. For instance, say, "Hello. Mr. Billings speaking."

- The next time you're in a group situation, force yourself to ask a question if you usually hesitate to do so. Pursuing greatness sometimes means doing things that at first feel uncomfortable but that, with practice, become second nature.

- When meeting new people, always smile. Be the first to extend your hand and introduce yourself. Make eye contact.

- Be a good listener. Give your undivided attention to the person speaking. Concentrate on what he or she is saying, not on what you're going to say next. To be a good listener, listen with your heart.

- Accept compliments graciously, with a simple "thank you." People who downplay compliments don't think much of themselves. Likewise, people who boast about their accomplishments also lack self-esteem. Both an inferiority complex and a superiority complex are signs of a low self-image.

- Don't make excuses for your shortcomings. Always think positively about yourself, and always speak positively about your progress toward becoming a better person.

- Don't tell other people your problems unless, of course, you are seeking their specific advice. Most people will tune you out. Unfortunately, the average person is too self-centered to care about your problems. He's too wrapped up in his own.

- Never stop learning. Read books and listen to tapes that will help you to grow in self-love and self-esteem. Especially read the Bible on which all good success books are ultimately based.

- Take care of your body. Exercise. Get enough rest. Eat the right foods. Good health goes hand in hand with a good self-image and success in life.

- Take care of your mind. Do not allow negative thoughts to take root there. Get rid of bitterness, unforgiveness, jealousy, envy, lust, fear, and greed. These will always rob you of the success God wants you to have and will keep you from achieving greatness.

- Associate with successful people. Observe the way they relate to others, the way they think, speak, and act. Develop their good qualities in your own life. Remember that "as iron sharpens iron, so one man sharpens another" (Proverbs 27: 17 NIV).

- Be gentle on yourself. Allow yourself some time to do what you want to do. Be flexible and learn to laugh at yourself. Learn to be a giver, especially of yourself. This is the secret of living, for "he that watereth shall be watered also himself" (Proverbs 11: 25 KJV).

Talking to Yourself

Positive self-talk plays a crucial role in the development of a healthy self-image. Tell yourself every day that you are special and important, that you were created for success, that you can become anything you want to be. At first you may feel ridiculous. Thoughts like "Who do you think you are?" may cross your mind. Push them aside and keep telling yourself that you are somebody. After a while, you will begin to believe what you are saying, and, eventually, you will become what you are saying.

When I first began to write seriously, I would tell myself, "I am a writer." People would ask me what my profession was, and I would respond, "I'm a writer." At first, I nearly choked on the words. "Whom are you trying to kid?" a voice would whisper in my mind. But I refused to listen to that voice. Instead, I kept telling myself that I am a writer. After a few months, I really believed it. Today, I feel perfectly comfortable knowing that I am truly called by God to be a writer.

All of your actions will be consistent with your self-image. Let's look at a common illustration of this truth.

Most women believe that they are incapable of proficiency in mathematics. Haven't you heard the comment, "I don't have a mind for math"? Most likely, it was a woman who made such a comment.

Why do most women believe that they are weak in math? Because mathematical proficiency is inconsistent with their self-image. Perhaps this belief arises from cultural and educational systems that have traditionally considered math "a man's subject" requiring the logical prowess usually associated with men rather than with women.

Whatever the reason, women consistently score lower than men in nationwide math tests. Why? Not because women have inferior minds when it comes to math, but because they believe they have inferior minds. The mind of a woman is as capable of mastering mathematics as is the mind of a man. But a woman's poor self-image in regard to math will usually not allow her to succeed in this traditionally male field. Only if and when she changes her self-image about mathematics will a woman be able to do as well as a man.

This principle applies to every area of life. If you want to change failure actions into success actions, you must first change your self-image. Once you have a better concept of yourself, you will attract those things and those situations consistent with your improved self-image. Like a magnet, you will draw to yourself all the elements necessary for success in your chosen endeavor.

Decide right now to accept yourself by improving your self-image through positive self-talk. You owe it to yourself. As you do, you will be taking a giant step forward toward becoming great.

Chapter Ten

Forgiving Yourself

Doctors are discovering that many physical ailments, such as arthritis, colitis, and headaches, are often the result of unforgiveness. Of all the deterrents to self-love, unforgiveness is perhaps the greatest. I would venture to say that unforgiveness has caused more failure and more illness in life than any other sin. Like an ugly cancer, it eats at the very heart of the person who refuses to forgive.

Unforgiveness may be two-fold: toward others and toward yourself. If not checked and uprooted, both types of unforgiveness will destroy you.

Many Christians face challenges in the area of unforgiveness because they do not fully understand what it means to forgive. Like love, forgiveness is a decision, not a feeling. By a deliberate act of your will, you choose to forgive.

But not only do you choose to forgive; you choose to forget as well. Forgiving is only half of the process; forgetting is the other half. Many Christians miss it in the forgetting part. How often have you heard the comment, "I'll forgive, but I can't forget"? This is not true forgiveness.

When we confess our sins to God the Father, He forgets as well as forgives. Isaiah 43: 25 TLB states: "I, yes, I alone am He who blots away your sins for my own sake and will never think of them again." We too must forget after we have forgiven.

After you've decided to forgive, Satan will continue to harass you with feelings of bitterness and resentment. When he does, just remind him, in the Name of Jesus, of your decision to forgive and of your determination to stand on that decision no matter what you feel. You will soon discover that the negative feelings have disappeared.

Some people have no difficulty forgiving others but great difficulty forgiving themselves. I'm one of those people. Being of a perfectionistic temperament, I tend to be hard on myself.

Once, while I was struggling with forgiving myself for some negative words I had spoken, the Lord lovingly chastised me with these words: "Who are you not to forgive yourself when I Who am God have forgiven you?" I decided then and there to forgive myself and to get on with my life.

Forgiving yourself means accepting your humanity. It means being gentle with yourself and knowing that, with God's help, you can overcome any weakness. It means forgetting the past and accepting God's promise in I John 1: 9 that if you confess your sins, He is faithful and just to forgive you and to cleanse you of all unrighteousness.

Decide now to forgive others and to forgive yourself. It is a crucial part of becoming great.

Chapter Eleven

Discovering the Real You

Who are you? Oh, I know you can say, "I'm John Doe, an accountant with CPA Associates," or "I'm Mary Jones, a computer programmer with Motivengine, Inc." But who are you really deep down where you live? When the masks of daily living are removed, who is left in the solitude of stark sincerity?

Several years ago I attended a Christian seminar on relationships. One of the speakers challenged us with a thought-provoking piece of writing which I would like to share with you:

> Don't be fooled by me. Don't be fooled by the face I wear. I wear a mask. I wear a thousand masks—masks that I am afraid to take off; and none of them are me. Pretending is an art that is second nature to me, but don't be fooled. I give the impression that I am secure, that all is sunny and unruffled within me as well as without; that confidence is my name and coolness my game, that the water is calm and I am in command; and that I need no one. But don't believe me, please. My surface may seem smooth, but my surface is my mask, my ever varying and ever concealing mask. Beneath lies no smugness, no complacence. Beneath dwells the real me in confusion, in fear, in aloneness. But I hide that. I don't want anybody to know it. I panic at the thought of my weakness and fear being exposed. That's why I frantically create a mask to hide behind
>
> —a nonchalant, sophisticated façade—to help me pretend, to shield me from the glance that knows. But such a glance is precisely my salvation, my only salvation, and I know it. That is, if it's followed by acceptance; if it's followed by love. It's the only thing that can liberate me

73

from myself, from my own self-built prison wall, from the barriers I so painstakingly erect. It's the only thing that will assure me of what I can't assure myself— that I am really something... Who am I, you may wonder. I am someone you know very well. I am every man you meet. I am every woman you meet. I am every child you meet. I am right in front of you. Please ... love me.

Author unknown

How wonderful it is to realize that "the glance that knows" for every person is the loving and forgiving glance of Jesus Christ! This is the only glance that brings salvation, and it is offered to all who would come to Him. When we surrender to that glance, we are free to remove every mask in the light of His unconditional love. We are free to discover who we really are.

But the discovery process is often very painful. It requires that you be willing to remove those masks that are keeping you from knowing yourself, knowing others, and knowing God. But you can do it! If you are willing to face the pain, you will reap the wonderful reward of freedom that comes from self-acceptance based on self-knowledge.

But how can you discover the real you? Two things are necessary:

1) You must want to discover real

2) You must be willing to be vulnerable.

Let's take a closer look at each of these points.

1. YOU MUST WANT TO DISCOVER THE REAL YOU. The achievement of any goal begins with a desire. In order for that goal to become a reality, desire must be accompanied by action. Desire without action will get you nowhere.

Too many people dream without putting legs on their dreams. But dreaming without acting to fulfill your dream is nothing more than wishful thinking. Like faith without works, it is dead (James 2: 17). In order to discover the real you, therefore, you must be willing to act on your dream.

Because you must know who you are before you can love yourself, discovering the real you lies at the basis of becoming great. Dr. Schuller puts it well when he says, "If you want to love yourself, you have to know yourself. You'll never know yourself until you are yourself" (*Self-Love*, p. 105).

Here are some ways in which you can discover the real you:

a) Through feedback from other people. To a great extent, we discover who we really are through feedback from other people. Examine the effect you have on people. Are you generally well-received? Do people like to be around you? Do they feel better about themselves after they have been with you? Or do they say, "He brightens up the whole room ... when he leaves"?

The reactions you create in others often tell you much about yourself. Sometimes, however, people will dislike you because you have the courage to stand up for your convictions. Even Jesus had enemies. In this kind of situation, however, God can cause even your enemies to be at peace with you (Proverbs 16: 7). Treating your enemies according to God's Word results in favor.

b) Through belonging to a family or group. Contributing to the functioning of a family or group makes you aware of your strengths and weaknesses. You discover what makes you impatient and what makes you feel relaxed. You learn what attitudes and actions irritate you, and what delight you. In the process, you also learn what areas of your life need improvement. Strong ties within a family or a group encourage self-discovery and enhance self-worth.

c) Through special friendships. Having a friend you can trust with your dreams and fears is an excellent means to self-discovery. Such friends provide a sounding board for your ideas and feelings. Moreover, a true friend will honestly tell you, when asked, what characteristics about you are pleasing and what are offensive. In sharing yourself with a special friend, you come to see yourself in a new dimension. Spouses should be this kind of friend to each other. There is nothing so fulfilling in a marriage relationship as having your spouse as your best friend.

d) Through involvement in a cause you deeply believe in. Often we discover ourselves through the action we take for a cause in which we believe. Until I became actively involved in the political process of this country, I was not fully aware of the depth of my convictions about freedom and free enterprise.

e) Through adversity. It is said that a man's true colors show in times of trouble. Perhaps you've experienced a crisis that required tremendous strength to overcome. After it was over, you may have been surprised at your courage during the trial. Adversity sometimes brings out strengths we never knew we had.

f) Through being creative. Lois had always had a desire to paint. Fearful, however, that she was not "artistically inclined," she never took a brush in hand. One day, in her mid-thirties, she finally decided to take a few oil painting lessons. To her great delight, she discovered that her life-long desire to paint indicated a talent for art.

I believe that a desire to do something signifies a latent talent in that area. If you've always had a desire to play the piano, very likely you have a talent for it. If you've always had the desire to build houses, you probably have a talent for architecture or carpentry.

g) Through risk-taking. You will never discover the real you until you are willing to take risks. The eaglet never knows he can fly until his mother pushes him out of the nest. At first he falls dangerously. Just as he is about to crash to the ground, his father swoops under him with his wide pinions and lifts him to safety. Before long, the eaglet is flying on his own.

So it is with you. You were created by God to be an eagle. But like the eaglet, you must leave the nest and spread your wings. You must be willing to surrender yourself to the air, just as a person learning to swim must be willing to surrender himself to the water.

But like the father eagle who is ever-present to catch his baby should he fall, so our heavenly Father is ever-present to catch you should you fall. He will not allow you to crash to the ground. As you surrender yourself to His care, He will lift you up. Soon you'll be flying fearlessly, knowing that through Him you can do all things.

2. YOU MUST BE WILLING TO BE VULNERABLE. Vulnerability is the quality of revealing your true thoughts and feelings regardless of the response of others. This is frightening for most people because it means ripping off the masks of status, strength, sophistication, superiority, self-sufficiency, and success, and risking rejection and ridicule for the greater goal of intimacy. But in the painful process of removing those masks, you will experience the exhilaration of discovering your true self.

When you allow yourself to be vulnerable, you draw people to you. Your transparency makes them feel that they aren't so different after all. Letting other people know that you too struggle with the problems common to all men causes them to feel close to you. It gives them hope that if you have overcome difficult situations, so can they.

If you never open up to people, they will feel uncomfortable and inferior around you.

Moreover, they will respond to your reticence in kind by not opening up to you.

Now I am not advocating total and unreserved exposure of situations that should remain confidential, such as marital or family matters. There are times for keeping some things to yourself. On the other hand, a willingness to share your struggles as well as your victories is a great aid to self-discovery.

The world so desperately needs the real you. God wants to use the real you to further His kingdom in the earth. Allow yourself to be vulnerable. In so doing, you will be true to yourself and really live.

Removing the Masks

Being vulnerable involves removing the masks you've worn for so long that you almost can't distinguish the mask from your real face. A mask that has been worn for years becomes painted on. The longer you've worn it, the more difficult it is to remove. But remove it you must if you want to discover who you really are.

What masks are you wearing? Ask yourself the following questions:

1) Do I use material things—such as money, clothes, cars—to measure my self-worth?
2) Am I afraid that others will reject me when they find out what I'm really like?
3) Am I afraid that if I discover who I really am, I won't like myself?
4) Am I more concerned with the outer me than with the inner me?

If you answered "yes" to any of these questions, you may be wearing a mask—or more than one. There are many different kinds of masks. Here are the most common:

1. *The mask of respectability.* This mask is also called the mask of social status. People who wear this mask use their position in society to keep others at a distance. The mask of respectability is characterized by aloofness. Those wearing this mask are often considered snobs. Interestingly enough, the mask of respectability is not always found among the traditionally wealthy. It is usually worn by people from poor backgrounds who have acquired a certain measure of success but have forgotten where they came from and who helped them to succeed.

2. *The mask of economic status.* The person wearing this mask bases his self-worth on money. The more money he has, the more important he thinks he is. Ironically, people wearing this mask usually struggle with financial problems but will never admit it.

3. *The mask of intelligence.* People wearing this mask flaunt their intelligence by employing verbose jargon in order to impress. On close examination, you will find that such people are usually not saying anything of great importance. More often than not, their words are meaningless.

4. *The mask of strength.* Those who wear this mask refuse to admit to any weakness nor will they ever ask for help. They are totally self-sufficient, sometimes to the point of arrogance. Such people are motivated by pride and by an inordinate fear of exposure. They live in a state of constant stress which becomes more accentuated because they bear it alone. Many so-called "macho" men fall into this category.

5. *The mask of perfection.* The person wearing this mask has a powerful need to be superior to others in everything he does. He is very critical of himself and often impatient with and critical of others. This person has difficulty accepting his humanity.

How can you remove the masks that are keeping you from discovering who you really are? Here are some suggestions:

a) *Listen carefully to criticism.* Honestly evaluate it to determine whether it applies to you or not. Even negative criticism can tell you things about yourself that you may not be aware of.

All of us have blind spots—those areas of weakness that others see but that we cannot see. Whenever you are criticized, consider the criticism objectively. You may be surprised at what you learn about yourself.

b) *Learn all you can about human behavior.* Most people are unaware of how they tick. Learning about why you act the way you do will help you to recognize the masks you may be wearing. It will also help you to understand other people and to help them in their personal growth.

c) *Study the Epistles of Paul.* He discusses at length the differences between the person led by his senses and the person led by the Holy Spirit. By studying these Epistles, you will discover why you do the things you don't want to do and why you don't do the things you want to do. You will learn how consistently to do the things you want to do by walking in God's Spirit.

Removing your masks is a freeing experience. In the process, you will find that not only will you be selling yourself on you, but you will be selling others on you too.

Losing Your Life to Find It

Ours is a narcissistic world which seeks self-gratification at the expense of love. Everywhere we turn, we hear cries for self-fulfillment at any cost. "Do your own thing" has become the catchphrase of modern-day psychology. Yet the world's way to self-fulfillment leads only to callous selfishness and greed which, in reality, are tantamount to idolatry.

The Word of God says that we are no longer our own. We have been bought with a price (I Corinthians 6: 19-20). Like the seed which must die before the plant can grow, so too must we die to ourselves before we can truly live.

If you want to find meaning in life, you must be willing to lay down your life for others. Jesus said, "Whoever loses his life for My sake will save it, but whoever insists on keeping his life will lose it; and what profit is there in gaining the whole world when it means forfeiting one's self?" (Luke 9: 24-25 TLB).

If you really want to discover yourself, become a servant. Jesus said, "To be the greatest, be a servant" (Matthew 23: 11 TLB). Being a servant means placing the needs of others before your own needs. It means putting aside your own interests for the good of others.

The greatest self-discovery lies in giving yourself away. Like the seed that surrenders itself to the soil to produce a fruit-bearing plant, so will you, in surrendering yourself to the service of others, produce a fruit-bearing life. It is a paradox. But as Christians we know that God's ways are not like the world's ways.

Your life is a seed. Unless it is planted in the lives of others, it will simply wither and die. Its potential will never be realized. But when you plant your life in the lives of others, it will multiply itself in ways you never expected. Once again the law of compensation operates. When you sow your life for others, you reap life for yourself.

When you refuse to give yourself away, you become stagnant. Consider the Jordan River. It flows into both the Dead Sea and the Sea of Galilee. But because the Dead Sea has no outlet, the water in it stagnates and putrefies. The Sea of Galilee, however, flows into other bodies of water. As a result, its water is fresh.

A self-contained life, bent on serving only its own ends, eventually dies. The life that allows the love of God to flow through it into others is continually replenished and flourishes.

Don't be like the Dead Sea. Allow your life to flow into others and experience the great reward of self-discovery. For it is in giving yourself away that you will find yourself.

Chapter Twelve

The Potter and the Clay

I am an occasional potter. Thanks to my generous husband, I have my own electric wheel and kiln. My experience with clay has taught me much about self-image.

Clay, when soft and pliable, will yield to the hands of the potter. In order to keep the clay pliant during the shaping process, potters continually use water.

One of the most critical moments in pottery occurs when centering the clay on the wheel. Once that center point is found, the clay will remain balanced, and your chances of producing a beautiful product will be good. If that point of balance is not achieved in the beginning, however, the clay must be removed from the wheel and the kneading process begun all over again.

Our lives are like clay. As we remain soft and pliable in God's hands, he can shape us into beautiful vessels. What keeps us soft is the water of His Word.

The clay centered on the wheel represents the life centered in God. When God is our center point, then our life is in balance. Every area of our life receives equal attention and remains under the control of God.

If, however, we remove God from the center of our life, then we get off balance. Consequently, God has to remove us from the wheel and begin the kneading process all over again.

Kneading involves pressure. But God can use that pressure to prepare us once again for the wheel.

The Yielded Spirit

You discover yourself when you yield to what God wants for your life. Surrendering to the Lord is not slavery; it's true freedom. It is allowing God to fashion you into the vessel He has designed you to be.

When you harden your heart to God's will for your life, you become like hardened clay which the potter cannot mold. When clay is hard, it either remains a lump, never achieving its potential, or it cracks into fragments.

Many people's lives have cracked and fragmented because they have been unwilling to yield to God's will for them. As you yield yourself to God, He can begin the shaping process in your life. During the process, you will discover who you really are. You will discover your greatness.

A Vessel of Honor

God's desire is that you be a vessel of honor fit for His table. You can be that vessel of honor by trusting yourself to the expert hands of the Potter Who created you in the first place.

Clay has many different properties, depending on where it is found. The experienced potter knows what properties will produce the effects he wishes to achieve. He knows that a particular kind of clay will be good for bowls, while another kind will work best for items of a more delicate nature.

So it is with God. He knows your temperament and personality. He knows what talents he has given you and how you can best develop those talents. By yielding to Him, you allow Him to take those talents and use them to the fullest for His glory.

Become the vessel of honor God wants to make of you. Choose to yield yourself to His hands. If you do, a surprising thing will happen. You will find that instead of having lost your identity, you will have found your only real identity that is in Jesus Christ.

Part IV

The Power of the Dream

Do you remember how you used to dream as a child? You had visions of flying to the moon, or of painting the most beautiful picture in the world, or of becoming the President of the United States.

Do you remember how excited you felt when thinking about your dream? In your mind's eye you could actually see yourself achieving it. Nothing could stand in your way.

But something happened on the way from childhood to adulthood. People began to laugh at you for being a dreamer. They told you that dreaming was impractical and inconsistent with reality. "Don't get your hopes up," they would say. "You'll only be disappointed." They told you to forget your dreams and get on with the practical things of life, like getting an education so that you could find a good job so that you could be successful.

So your dreams slowly began to fade. After all, these people were grown-ups. Surely they knew more about life than you did. They had experienced it. Perhaps dreams were only for storybooks anyway. Why should you get your hopes up if dreams couldn't come true?

So, instead of aiming for the presidency of the United States, you opted for a job on an assembly line. After all, who were you to think that you could become President of the United States? It took a famous name and money, and, of course, it depended on whom you knew. Finally, it was all a matter of luck anyway.

Instead of painting the world's most beautiful picture, you chose the security of a nine-to-five job programming a computer. Painting would never put food on the table. Moreover, being a painter was being out of touch with reality.

Now there's nothing wrong with assembly lines or computers. On the contrary, they are great inventions which have helped the world immeasurably. But if working on an assembly line or programming a computer is not your dream, then it is wrong for you. You're lying to yourself. You're not being true to the purpose for which God created you. You're on the wrong track. And unless you get on the right track, you'll never become great.

No human being finds happiness until he fulfills the purpose for which he was created. So many people are unhappy today because they are not fulfilling the purpose for which God created them. Your main reason for being is to love and enjoy God and to glorify Him in all that you do. If you do not know God personally through His Son Jesus Christ, you will never fulfill the primary purpose for which you were created.

The secondary reason for which you were created is to fulfill a special calling on this earth. A good way to determine your calling is to discover your talents. The talents God gave you are directly related to His purpose for you. When God calls you to do something, He always equips you to do it.

God has a dream for your life—a very big dream. He is the Master Dreamer, and because you are made in His image, you too are meant to dream. When your dreams line up with God's dreams for you, He is able to perform in you far above anything that you could ask or imagine (Ephesians 3: 20).

Everything around you is the result of a dream. The car you drive, the building you work in, the book you read—all began as someone's dream. The beauty of the world in which we live is the result of God's dream for man. In fact, God says in His Word that without a dream you will die (Proverbs 29: 18).

If you feel dead on the inside because you've given up your dream, I want to encourage you: "For there is hope for a tree—if it's cut down it sprouts again, and grows tender, new branches" (Job 14: 7 TLB). You can fan that flicker of hope still lingering within you. You can revive your dream. You can achieve it if you will but catch the vision of who you are in Jesus Christ.

Chapter Thirteen

Catching the Vision

Dreams are like butterflies. They flutter and fly in seemingly illusive patterns, often just barely beyond our reach. Too often, however, we allow them to escape.

Those dreams that God gave you are floating around in your mind, ever in danger of being snatched by Satan. "What makes you think that you could be debt-free?" he'll whisper. Or, "Whoever said that you have artistic talent?"

Unless you guard your dreams with the Word of God, you stand a good chance of losing them. The greatest battles you will ever wage will always take place in the six inches between your ears. It is here that Satan fights you to keep you from becoming all that God wants you to be. If you allow him to do so, Satan will keep you locked in a mental box for the rest of your life.

Get Out of Your Box

One of the wealthiest men in Seattle, Washington, died several years ago leaving behind a legacy of hope that has touched literally thousands of lives. At the age of two years, P. B. Burkland contracted polio. His legs shriveled up and he lost his ability to walk.

Not knowing what to do, P. B.'s parents placed him in a wooden box with a rope attached to one side so that they could pull him around the house. Day after day, the little boy heard comments like "He'll never walk again," "He'll never amount to much," "He probably won't live very long."

One day his parents parked his box in front of a mirror. By this time, P. B. had reached the age of seven. As he looked at himself in the mirror, he suddenly had a vision of himself standing up in the box.

With a burst of hope, he began to rock back and forth until the box tipped over. Rushing in to see what had caused the noise, P. B.'s mother scolded him and put him back in the box.

But the little boy would not give up. He rocked back and forth again until the box tipped over. Then he began to crawl across the room, dragging his shriveled legs behind him. After much struggle, he finally pulled himself up on his legs and began to walk again.

P. B. Burkland outlived every one of his relatives who had predicted his early demise. As he lay on his deathbed at the age of seventy-five, his parting words were: "I realized that I did not have to stay in the box. My mission in life has been to tell people that they don't have to stay in the box either."

Are you trapped in the box of poverty, sickness, inferiority, or fear? You don't have to stay in your box. Like P. B. Burkland, you can get out. All you have to do is believe that you can and then act on that belief.

The Bible says that all things are possible to him who believes (Mark 9: 23). Begin seeing yourself out of that box. Begin visualizing yourself as debt-free, or confident, or healed.

You are the only one keeping you in your box. Decide now to take God at His Word. You can do all things through Christ Who strengthens you (Philippians 4: 13).

You Were Made for Greatness

Joe Sorrentino was a city kid who grew up in one of the worst neighborhoods of Brooklyn. The son of a sanitation worker, Joe lived by the sword as the leader of a dreaded New York street gang. Quick with his fist, he was arrested and spent time in reform school.

In an attempt to straighten himself out, he joined the Marines but became so incorrigible that he was dishonorably discharged. At this point, Joe had a choice to make. He could either continue down the road of failure and destruction, or he could make an about-face in the direction of success. To his credit and to the good of humanity, Joe chose the latter.

He decided to better himself through education and graduated *magna cum laude* from the University of California. Re-enlisting in the Marines, he became the first person to be discharged honorably after an earlier dishonorable discharge. Joe went on to Harvard where he studied law and became one of the top leaders on campus. Today he serves as a juvenile court judge in California where he teaches delinquent children that they have the power to choose who they will become in life.

What made Joe Sorrentino, who had all the makings of a potentially hardened criminal, choose to turn his life around? When you read Joe's story, you learn of the great impact his seventh-grade teacher had on his life. It takes only one person to believe in you for you to realize that you can succeed. Joe Sorrentino had that one person in his seventh-grade teacher.

Look back over your life. Is there one particular person who stands out in your memory as someone who believed in you? Perhaps it was a coach, or an aunt, or an employer. Whoever it was, that person saw in you the potential for greatness.

You were made for greatness. You are the crowning glory of God's creation, the epitome of His creative love. You were made to rule and to reign under the Lordship of Jesus Christ. The Bible calls you a king and a priest (I Peter 2: 9).

In his inspiring book, *Seeds of Greatness* (Fleming H. Revell, 1983, p. 39), Dr. Denis Waitley explains: "... there will never be a person who is more important than any other person." Inside of you are seeds of greatness just waiting to germinate and to grow. But it's up to you to water them and to nourish them. Within you, programmed by God Himself, is a special dream, tailor-made just for you—a dream of who you are and where you fit into God's plan.

Discovering God's dream for you is the key to achieving greatness. When you realize who you are and why you are here on this earth, your life will acquire a meaning and a purpose that will give you great joy. No longer will you dread getting up in the morning; you'll be eager to. No longer will you fall into bed at night exhausted with depression; you'll fall into bed exhausted with satisfaction from a day full of positive effort toward your goals.

Get excited about yourself. You are made in the image of God. No other creature—not even the angels—can claim this great honor. Don't let God down by settling for less than you really are. He believes in you. After all, He made you. And who knows better than He who you are and what you can achieve?

Take a second look at yourself and decide now that you'll never again put yourself down. Become your own best friend. Trust in God and you'll see Him do in your life what you never believed possible (Ephesians 3: 20).

Chapter Fourteen

Imagining the Vision

As I was growing up, there was a lot of talk among educators about IQ, or Intelligence Quotient. Your IQ was supposedly an indication of how smart you were.

I recall taking IQ tests every couple of years in school. The results were always kept secret. There was a general fear that having a low IQ was worse than having a dread disease. It was rumored among the students that only those with high IQ's would make it big in life—whatever that meant.

Although the IQ test results were kept secret, we students could tell who were the smart ones and who were the stupid ones. The smart kids were directed into the college preparatory courses, while those with supposedly lesser intelligence ended up in business courses.

Why business courses were considered easier, I'll never know. At any rate, through some inexplicable educational maneuver, success became linked with the college-bound. Those who chose to work after graduation from high school—well, their IQ's must have been low.

Such misconceptions on the part of educators led to a sad loss of tremendous human potential. The truth is that your IQ (Intelligence Quotient) has little to do with your success. Your IQ (Imagination Quotient), on the other hand, has everything to do with it.

Dr. Maxwell Maltz says this of the imagination: "We act, or fail to act, not because of 'will,' as is commonly believed, but because of imagination. A human being always acts and feels and performs in accordance with what he imagines to be true about himself and his environment" (*Psycho-Cybernetics*, p. 31).

If you imagine and believe yourself to be a failure, than that's how you will act. If, on the other hand, you imagine yourself to be a success, then you will act like one.

Like a magnet, you will attract to yourself whatever you think about most. If failure thoughts dominate your mind, then you will attract failure. If success thoughts dominate your mind, then you will attract success.

Have you ever known anyone who always attracted good luck? Someone who always got all the breaks? Well, it wasn't luck at all. It was positive thinking, positive imaging, and plain hard work.

Since your mind is so designed that you will always gravitate toward your most dominant thought, it is crucial that your most dominant thoughts be those that move you toward the attainment of your God-given dreams. Let's take a look at how this works.

What Is Your IQ (Imagination Quotient)?

With what kind of mental pictures have you been filling your mind? Are they pictures that will draw you closer to God and, consequently, to success? Or are they pictures that damage your self-esteem and lead you to failure? Remember: what you think about is what you will become in life.

Your mind, like a torpedo, will seek the target you program it to seek. This is called the principle of psycho-cybernetics.

Cybernetics is the science that deals with the comparative study of automatic control systems. When this science is applied to a study of the human brain, it is called "psycho-cybernetics."

The word "cybernetics" comes from the Greek word meaning "the steersman." Dr. Maltz compares the human mind to a servo-mechanism, a device that achieves its goal through a method of positive and negative feedback (See *Psycho-Cybernetics*, pp. 19-21).

Watch a baby learning to feed himself. His first effort to get the spoon into his mouth results in a mouthful of food right in his eye. On the next try, he may hit his nose. Finally, sifter several attempts refined through negative feedback, he does get the spoonful of food into his mouth.

The same process occurs in learning to play an instrument or to play basketball. Your first attempts will be off target and result in negative feedback. As you practice, however, you come closer and closer to the target. In essence, you are refining your maneuvers based on the negative feedback you are receiving. As Dr. Maltz points out: "It is characteristic of all learning that as learning takes place, correction becomes more and more refined" (ibid., p. 21).

In the case of the baby learning to feed himself, his dominant thought is to get that food into his mouth. The musician's dominant thought is to hit the right notes, and the basketball player's dominant thought is to make those baskets. In all three instances, imaging is involved. The baby sees himself getting that food into his mouth; the musician sees himself playing the right notes; and the basketball player sees himself making those baskets. Through repeated effort and persistence, all three eventually achieve their goals.

Stop right now and jot down some of the thoughts you dwelt upon during the last hour. Were they thoughts of worry about your finances, your spouse, your children, your health? Or were they thoughts of victory over a particular problem or situation?

Thoughts that do not move you toward your goals are counterproductive. Not only do such thoughts keep you from achieving your goals, but they also move you toward the death of your dreams.

You alone are responsible for your thoughts. What you think about most will, indeed, come to pass in your life.

Jacob's Flocks: the Power of Visualization

Imaging, as Dr. Norman Vincent Peale explains in his book by that title (*Guideposts*, 1982, p. 17), "is the forming of mental pictures or images." He goes on to say that imaging "is based on the principle that there is a deep tendency in human nature to ultimately become precisely like that which we imagine or image ourselves as being" (ibid.).

So powerful is this principle that even animals respond to it. In the biblical account of Jacob's flocks, we have a dynamic illustration of the principle of imaging. Jacob had agreed to continue working for his father-in-law Laban on the condition that Laban give him a particular portion of his flock. When Laban consented, Jacob deceived him. The Biblical passage follows:

> Then Jacob took fresh shoots from poplar, almond, and plane trees, and peeled white streaks in them, and placed these rods beside the watering troughs so that the flocks would see them when they came to drink; for that is when they mated. So the flocks mated before the white-streaked rods, and their offspring were streaked and spotted, and Jacob added them to his flock. Then he divided out the ewes from Laban's flock and segregated them from the rams and let them mate only with Jacob's black rams. Thus he built his flocks from Laban's. Moreover, he watched for the stronger animals to mate, and placed the peeled branches before them, but didn't with the feebler ones. So the less healthy lambs were Laban's and the stronger ones were Jacob's! As a result, Jacob's flocks increased rapidly and he became very wealthy, with many servants, camels, and donkeys" (Genesis 30: 37-43 TLB).

Those sheep had continually before them an image of how Jacob wished them to reproduce.

And that's exactly how they reproduced.

Most Christian children are familiar with the song "Be Careful, Little Eyes, What You See." What you look at on a continual basis will become imbedded in your mind and affect your actions. We have only to consider the rise in violent crimes since the influx of pornography into our society. Television, also, has contributed greatly to the moral breakdown of America. You are what you think about, and what you think about comes from what you see and what you hear.

But that same power of visualization that causes heartbreak and failure can also make you a success in life. How? Let me tell you of a personal experience.

During my freshman year in college, I joined the Modern Foreign Language Club. I was in love with languages and with the wonderful opportunity they offered for touching lives.

At the very first meeting, I set for myself the goal to be president of the Foreign Language Club in my senior year. I had no idea how I was going to achieve that goal. But one thing I knew for sure: I would be president in my senior year.

For three years, I saw myself as president, carrying out the duties of that office. I envisioned myself conducting meetings, speaking before groups, hosting visiting dignitaries. I experienced in advance the excitement of leading others with common interests. As you've probably guessed, I was indeed elected president of the Modern Foreign Language Club in my senior year.

Without understanding the process of imaging, I had practiced it for three years before achieving my goal. I had engaged in what Dr. Denis Waitley calls "pre-play" or "simulation," just as the astronauts "simulated" or "pre-played" their flight to the moon.

Returning POWs tell of remarkable results from imaging. While in the "Hanoi Hilton," many of them became fine musicians, golfers, and athletes without ever having left their cells. Through mental imaging of his golf game, one POW scored a 76 only one week after his return to the United States. It was his first time on the green in five years.

Once, while attending a musicians' conference, I spoke to a concert cellist who does most of his practicing on the subway—without his instrument. In his mind's eye, he rehearses over and over again and images himself as never making a mistake.

In your mind, you can always perform flawlessly. If you do it right in your mind again and again, you will do it right in real life.

Get a mental picture of what you want to be. Spend at least five minutes a day thinking about that image. Find a quiet spot where you can close your eyes, turn on some soft music, and relax. See yourself making that big sale or receiving that gold medal.

When imaging, it is important that you look at the image through your own eyes, not someone else's. For example, see the crowds cheering as you walk up to the podium to receive your company's top sales award or that coveted football letter. Imagine the lights, the plants on the stage, the smiles on the people's faces. Feel the butterflies in your stomach, the pounding in your heart, the lightness in your step. Taste the sweetness of success.

If you imagine your success for a few moments each day and add the essential ingredients of consistent effort and persistence, that which you imagine will become a reality.

Developing Your Imagination Quotient

But perhaps you're not sure what to imagine or how to go about it. Perhaps you consider yourself a person without an imagination.

Let me simply say that everyone has an imagination. Some are more developed than others, but everyone has one. If you worry, you have an imagination. But your imagination is directed toward the wrong goal. It is a fear-dominated imagination. You need to change it to a faith-dominated one.

Like a muscle, your imagination can be developed. With proper use and exercise, it can bring you great success. Let me help you attain that success. If you're willing, the best is yet to come.

Dare to Dream Big!

Have you ever asked a five-year-old what she wants to be when she grows up? Perhaps she said something like "I'm going to be a doctor and make sick people well," or "I'm going to invent a new kind of car that flies just above the ground at 200 miles an hour."

Children are master dreamers. Fresh from the heart of God, they have not yet lost their belief in the seemingly impossible. Nothing is beyond their reach.

And so it should be with those of us who are the children of God. Doesn't He say in His Word that unless we become like little children, we shall not enter the kingdom of heaven (Mark 10: 15)? Doesn't He also say that with Him, all things are possible (Matthew 19: 26)?

Notice that word "all." God said all things, not some. Elsewhere He says that you can do all things through Christ Who strengthens you (Philippians 4: 13). Do you truly believe that?

So many people who call themselves Christians live as though God's Word were not true. But if God says that all things are possible if you believe and that you can do all things through Christ, we had better take God at His Word and act on it.

There's the key: *act on it*. Faith without works is dead (James 2: 17). How can we say we have faith when our actions indicate otherwise?

In an earlier chapter, we discussed the "As-If Principle," the principle of speaking of those things that are not as if they were. Imaging and the "As-If Principle" work hand in hand.

When you dare to dream big, you are stretching your imagination. You are imagining those things that do not yet exist in the physical realm as though they already existed there. As you begin to visualize your goals and speak about them as though you had already attained them, you will surely see their fulfillment.

What is your biggest dream? Whatever it is, you can achieve it through imaging and work. Do you want to own a fleet of trucks and become the largest shipping firm in America? You can if you believe you can. Do you want to be the president of your corporation? You can if you believe you can. Do you want to be "Mother of the Year"? You can if you believe you can.

Beat Your Own Drum

Next to losing your soul for eternity, the worst tragedy that could befall you would be for you to die with your song still imprisoned within you. God gave you a song to sing, and unless you sing it, the world will suffer irreparable loss. It's up to you to find out what that song is and then to sing it.

Let me share with you some lessons I learned in the process of finding my own song:

1. *Determine what your talents are.* Your talents are the key to the song God created you to sing. There are three reliable indicators of a talent:

   a) A talent is an ability you enjoy exercising.

   b) A talent is an ability others recognize in you

   c) A talent is an ability that you can exercise with relative ease, although its development usually requires training and practice.

Numerous psychological tests are available that will help you to determine your talents. Many people experience restlessness and frustration simply because they are not aware of their talents and, consequently, have not developed them.

1. *Experiment with new activities.* Until I tried oil painting, I never thought I had any artistic talent. Now I'm hooked. I've discovered that I do indeed have artistic talent, and its expression through oil painting has given me great pleasure, enhanced my self-esteem, and brought pleasure to others. I'm a happier, freer person as the result of expressing myself through art.

2. *Don't let other people put you down.* If you want to try hang gliding, go to it. If you want to be your city's chess champion, go for it. As Shakespeare said, "'to thine own self be true."

Your drumbeat is different from everyone else's. The world needs your drum in the band. Be the best drummer you can be by being the best dreamer you can be. Remember: a big dreamer achieves big dreams by beating his own drum. If your drum is in tune with the Chief Drummer, then you'll never go wrong. Dream big, for with God all things are possible.

Chapter Fifteen

Writing the Vision

The Holy Bible is the written account of God's dream for mankind. Throughout the Word, there are several places where God commands us to write. Psychologically, the process of writing etches information into the mind in a way that hearing does not do.

Writing aids in focusing your thoughts. It helps you to organize your thinking and to concentrate on what is important. It helps you better to see the various aspects of a particular situation or problem.

You may have big dreams floating around in your head, but until you write them down, they are not really concrete. When you take pencil in hand and begin to write your dreams on paper, they suddenly take on a new dimension of possibility. They begin to take on flesh, the flesh of the written word which will eventually become the flesh of the realized dream.

Writing your dream preserves it in tangible form. It establishes a point of contact between you and the realization of your dream. The paper on which you write your dream becomes the launching pad for the fulfillment of your dream.

Launching Your Dream

Have you ever noticed the relative ease with which spacecraft leave the launching pad at Cape Canaveral? They just seem to lift effortlessly off the ground toward their predetermined destination. Years of preparation precede the great moment of launching. But all those years would be meaningless if the rocket were not supplied with fuel for the lift-off and journey.

While on the ground, the rocket is simply the vehicle for the fulfillment of the dream of conquering space. But nothing can happen until the rocket is launched.

The same is true of your dream. If you merely leave it on the launching pad without supplying it with fuel, it will never get off the ground. The fuel that launches your dream is action. But before you take action, you must know where you are going and what you need to do to get there. You must, in short, chart your course.

Charting Your Course through Goal-Setting

Goal-setting is an absolute pre-requisite for the achievement of success. Unfortunately, only ten percent of the people in the world have definite goals. Of those ten percent, only three percent write them down. Significantly, of the three percent who write down their goals, virtually all of them achieve them.

By setting goals, you will more readily move toward greatness. Goal-setting gives you a sense of purpose, of control over your life. Your confidence rises because you are making things happen instead of letting them happen. Suddenly you find that you have more energy. You are more excited about life. There's a lightness in your step that wasn't there before. For the first time, you know where you're going.

People who set goals and work toward them are healthier and happier. Listen to what Dr.

Maxwell Maltz says about goals:

> We are engineered as goal-seeking mechanisms. We are built that way. When we have no personal goal which we are interested in and means something to us, we have to go around in circles, feel lost and find life itself aimless and purposeless. We are built to conquer environment, solve problems, achieve goals and we find no real satisfaction or happiness in life without obstacles to conquer and goals to achieve. People who say that life is not worthwhile are really saying that they themselves have

no personal goals which are worthwhile. Get yourself a goal worth working for. Better still, get yourself a project. Decide what you want out of a situation. Always have something to look forward to (*Psycho-Cybernetics*, pp. 57-58).

But suppose you've never set goals. Where do you begin? The following steps will help you:

1. Pray. Tell God that you have decided to set some goals for your life and that you need His direction. Commit your goal-setting to Him, and He will establish your thoughts according to His will (Proverbs 16:3).

2. Set aside about two hours for your goal-setting session. Spend the first hour clarifying your values. Ask yourself, "What is most important to me in life?" The following list may jog your thinking:

a) My relationship with God
b) My relationship with my spouse
c) My relationship with my children
d) Winning souls for Christ
e) Health and physical fitness
f) Financial security
g) My job
h) Being active in my church
i) Continuing my education
j) Owning a home
k) Travel

Whatever you value most, write down. The following questions may help you to determine what really is important to you:

1. If I already had all the money I would ever want for the rest of my life, how would I spend my time? Would I continue to work at my job without pay?

2. If I had only one week left to live, with whom would I spend it?

3. If I could spend every day doing exactly what I want to do, what would I do?

Honestly answering questions like these forces you to think about what you really want to do with your life. It is important that you face such questions in setting your goals. Most people spend their lives doing what they have to do, not what they want to do. This is a major cause of many illnesses and the source of much stress and frustration.

Another way to determine what is important to you is to become aware of what you think about most during the day. When God was calling me into the writing ministry, I began to grow more and more dissatisfied with my job. It became increasingly difficult for me to keep my mind on my work. All I wanted to do was write.

The desire to write grew stronger and stronger. Finally, I had to face it squarely. Was I going to follow my dream, or was I going to spend the rest of my life suppressing it and succumbing to the negative consequences that result from stifling one's dream?

I chose to follow my dream. Ever since, I have felt truly fulfilled because I have discovered my calling in life. My prayer is that you too will have the courage to follow your dream and, in so doing, discover your purpose in life.

Now that you've written down what you value most in life, ask yourself these questions:

1. Do my values line up with the Word of God?

2. Do my values serve the well-being of others?

If you answered "yes" to these two questions, you are ready to begin the goal-setting process.

As you set your goals, keep in mind your most important values. Take each value you listed and ask yourself what goals will help move you toward the development of those values.

For example, if you listed as a value the improvement of your relationship with your spouse, write down specific goals that will help you to better that relationship. Here are some examples:

1) Go out to lunch once a week with my spouse.

2) Compliment my spouse at least three times a day.

3) Listen more attentively to my spouse.

4) Be more helpful.

5) Pray daily for my spouse.

After you've made a list of goals for each of your most important values in life, you will need to set a date for the achievement of your goals.

When setting goals, be flexible. Remember that goals are guidelines. As you grow in the Lord, He may reveal to you a new direction that He wants you to take. At that point, you will need to modify your goals. So relax when writing down your goals. They are not cast in concrete.

Goals are divided into three main categories: short-range, intermediate, and long-range. Let's take a close look at each category.

Short-Range Goals

Short-range goals are those goals that you would like to achieve within a year. They may be goals like losing thirty pounds, owning a new car, or completing a particular project. It is helpful to set these goals according to the calendar year, if possible.

Each year at the end of December, I spend several hours evaluating the previous year and setting my goals for the new year. I then take these yearly goals and break them down into monthly goals.

Just before each new month begins, I list my goals for that month, breaking them down into weekly goals. At the end of each week, I go one step farther: I list my goals for the following week, breaking them down into daily goals. Finally, before I go to bed each night, I make a list of my goals for the next day.

Let me emphasize an important point here. Throughout the entire goal-setting process, I continually review the goals I wish to accomplish during the year. This keeps them fresh in my mind so that I consciously direct my activities toward the achievement of my goals.

When setting short-range goals, be specific. For instance, it is not enough to say that you have a goal of drawing closer to God. You must list specific steps that will move you toward that goal. For example:

1) Spend one hour a day in prayer.

2) Read one chapter of the Bible daily.

Short-range goals are the building blocks for intermediate and long-range goals. Short-range goals are important because you can experience results in a short period of time. These successes along the way encourage you toward the attainment of your intermediate and long-range goals.

Intermediate Goals

Intermediate goals are those goals that you plan to accomplish within five years. When setting intermediate goals, decide first where you want to be in five years. Ask yourself these questions:

1) What kind of work will I want to be doing?

2) How much money will I want to be earning?

3) What will my relationship with God be like?

4) What will my relationship with my spouse be like?

5) What will my relationship with my children be like?

6) What kind of house will I be living in?

7) Will I be in better physical condition than I am now?

After you've decided where you want to be in five years, write down your goals and date them. Keep them in a conspicuous place so that you can read them aloud every day.

Long-Range Goals

Long-range goals are those that you plan to accomplish either by the end of your life or by a particular age, such as seventy-five or eighty. Or you may decide to complete them within a predetermined number of years, such as twenty-five. Whatever the case, make an effort to set long-range goals.

Some people have difficulty projecting themselves more than five years into the future. If you're one of those people, work on short-range and intermediate goals for now. As you become experienced with these, you will find it much easier to set long-range goals.

When setting long-range goals, imagine yourself looking back on your entire life. How would you like people to remember you? What contributions would you like to have made to the world? What personal and professional accomplishments would you like to have achieved?

Goal-setting is an exercise in creativity under the wonderful guidance of the Holy Spirit.

While you need to have big dreams, keep in mind the following points when setting goals:

1. *Be realistic.* For example, if you have a goal to lose fifty pounds, don't expect to lose it all in two days. It took some time to put all that weight on; it will take some time to get it off.

2. *Be patient.* Reaching your goals takes time. Sometimes it will look as though you're going backward instead of forward. It is especially during these times that you need to hold on to your dream. Everyone experiences setbacks in working toward goals.

3. *Be persistent.* Every day do something that will move you toward your goals. When making your daily list of things to do, assign top priority to those activities that will cause you to progress toward your goals. Always remain in the creative stage. When you must take care of things in the management area, delegate as much as possible. If you must do certain things yourself, leave them for later in the day.

4. *Be excited!* You deserve a round of applause. You are among the very small minority of people who set goals and achieve them. You are a winner through and through! When you are enthusiastic about your goals, you release the energy necessary to attain them. It is interesting to note that the word "enthusiasm" comes from the Greek word meaning "in God."

Once you have written down your goals, keep them constantly before you. Read them in the morning as you begin your day. Read them at regular intervals throughout the day: while waiting for a traffic light to change, while driving through a bank line, while waiting for an appointment. Read your goals again at night before you go to bed.

Continual visualization of your goals will propel you toward their achievement.

Chapter Sixteen

Fulfilling the Vision

The journey toward the fulfillment of your dream will be one of ups and downs, of hills and valleys. But don't be discouraged. Detours along the way are merely tests of your faith. Besides, the detours will often take you down roads whose beauty you never would have seen had you not taken those detours.

I recall a trip I once took to Washington, D.C. As I approached the city, I missed my exit on the Beltway. Because I was unfamiliar with the area, I had to continue for several miles before finding a safe place to turn around.

By this time it was evening. As I turned around to get back in the right direction, I witnessed the most beautiful sunset I had ever seen in my life. The sky was radiant with hues of purple, crimson, and orange. It was truly a breath-taking sight.

When I saw the sunset, I thanked God that I had missed the exit. The sunset was worth far more than the extra miles I had to drive.

Life is much the same way. When setbacks occur, you can either complain or you can look for the serendipity in them. You will enjoy life more when you look for the serendipities. Life is truly exciting for those who want it to be.

Every day can be a great day if you make it one. People often say to me, "Have a good day!" While I appreciate their kind wishes, my response is always, "Thank you. I'll make it one."

You too can make every day a great day. You too can fulfill the vision God gave you. Begin now. Time won't wait.

Predicting Your Future

Your future lies in your mouth. Where you will be in five years depends on what you're speaking today. Put a bridle on that tongue of yours and begin to speak success.

Start talking to yourself as though you've already reached your goal. For example, if you want to earn $100,000 a year, start saying, "It feels wonderful to be earning $100,000 a year." If you want to be in excellent physical shape, start saying, "I'm in great physical shape." Whatever you desire, start speaking it.

It's important to remember, however, that talking alone won't get you what you want. You have to take action to back up your talking. You can't just talk the talk; you have to walk the walk as well.

Passing through Valleys

Dr. Robert Schuller often says, "When the going gets tough, the tough get going." In your journey toward your dream, you will pass through valleys. There will be times when everything seems to be falling apart, or when nothing seems to be happening. Doubts will assail you and pressure you to quit.

It's during these "valley times" that you need to hold on the most tightly. Every successful person knows that failure is a part of success. If your attitude toward failure is that of a winner, you will view failure as simply a steppingstone to success. If, on the other hand, you consider failure as final, you will not get up and go at it again.

God knew that we would be passing through valleys at different times in our lives. In Psalm 23 we read these comforting words of encouragement: "Though I walk through the valley of the shadow of death, I will fear no evil: for thou art with me."

When you realize that your success is grounded in God, you will no longer fear the valleys. Instead, you will view a valley as merely the prelude to another mountain at the top of which lies success.

Let the valleys of life make you stronger. In the valleys, you'll find grass to feed on and water to drink if you look to Jesus, the Lord of the Valleys.

God's Timetable

Some of us have a longer valley to cross than others. God knows how much testing we need to make us strong. He knows how much training we need to take on the responsibility of the call that He has placed upon our lives. God's payday may not always be Friday, but it's always on time.

When we patiently allow God's plan to unfold in our lives, we experience a deeply rooted sense of peace. While we work as though success depended totally on us, we pray as though it depended totally on God.

There is a season for everything in life. There is a time to sow and a time to reap. If you have sown faithfully, you will surely reap. Keep your eyes on Jesus. The rest will take care of itself.

Eagles Fly High

Before we can learn how to walk, we must learn how to stand. Our valley experiences are times of learning how to stand. As we master the art of standing, we can then take on the challenge of learning how to walk, how to run, and, finally, how to fly.

But learning to walk, to run, and to fly requires a price. Once we have made the decision to pay the price, we will begin to move in the direction of success.

An insightful analogy can be made between the Christian and the eagle. In his enlightening book, *The Eagle Christian* (Old Faithful Press, 1984, p. 56), Kenneth Price writes:

> The eagle, unlike other birds, does not wing flight by batting his wings for he knows that his ability to fly is not the result of his own strength but rather a gift of God. The eagle mounts the wind much the same way one mounts a

horse and takes the reins in hand and controls his direction. Although he is subject to the wind, he also knows how to use the wind to reach some predetermined place.

As Christians, we too need to realize that our ability to succeed—our ability to fly—is not the result of our own strength but rather a gift from God. As the eagle mounts the wind in order to fly high, so too must we mount the winds of adversity in order to succeed. As the eagle uses the wind to reach his destination, so too must we use the winds of adversity to reach our predetermined goals.

You are an eagle! Lift up your wings and soar! Stay plugged into God through prayer and worship, for "they that wait upon the Lord shall renew their strength. They shall mount up with wings like eagles; they shall run and not be weary; they shall walk and not faint" (Isaiah 40: 31 TLB).

Part V

Choosing To Be A Giant

Olympic fans well remember Wilma Rudolph. Who would have ever thought that a little girl in leg braces would one day not only be the first woman to win three gold medals in track and field, but to do so in world record time?

As an infant, Wilma contracted polio which left her with a crooked left leg and an inwardly twisted left foot. Always a dreamer, she would spend the time traveling from her hometown of Clarksville, Tennessee, to Nashville for physical therapy imagining herself free of those braces.

When her doctor advised her to exercise her legs through daily massaging, Wilma took his advice one step farther. Every day, she would remove her braces and walk around the house for extended periods of time. After several months of such exercise, she was able to get rid of the leg braces once and for all.

But Wilma's dream didn't stop there. At the age of twelve, she decided to become an athlete. When her older sister tried out for the girls' basketball team, Wilma tried out too. She became a token player, warming the bench for nearly three straight seasons. As Wilma recounts in her autobiography, "I think the coach ... kept me around just because of my sister" (*Wilma*, New American Library, 1977, p. 42).

Undaunted, however, Wilma pressed on. She finally got up from the bench and into the action. Her playing caught the eye of Ed Temple, occasional referee for Wilma's games and well-known coach of the Tennessee State University Tigerbelles, the famed women's track team. When Temple asked for volunteers from the basketball team to try out for track, Wilma agreed.

She soon discovered that she had a special talent for running. At age fourteen, she joined the Tigerbelles and began serious training as a runner.

Through her participation in the Tigerbelles, Wilma met Mae Faggs, a former Olympic contender. Mae took Wilma under her wing and prepped her for the 1956 Olympic Games in Australia.

Although Wilma was eliminated in the semi-finals of the 200-meter dash at the 1956 games, she did win a bronze medal for finishing third in the women's 400- meter relay. She determined to shoot for the gold in 1960.

For the next four years, Wilma put herself through a training program that would have discouraged some of the best. But her persistence paid off. In 1960, cheered on by faithful fans, she became the first woman in the history of the Olympic Games to win three gold medals in field and track. The little girl in leg braces had become a world class athlete.

What made Wilma Rudolph stand out above the crowd? Her dream and her decision to act on that dream. Wilma chose to be a giant and she became one.

Chapter Seventeen

The Privilege of Choice

The freedom to choose is the greatest privilege given to us by our Creator. It is what differentiates us from animals and places us at the pinnacle of God's creation. But while the freedom to choose is a wonderful privilege, it can also be a dangerous one if we make the wrong choices.

In His Word, God has instructed us in the use of our privilege of choice. In Deuteronomy 30: 19 NIV He says, "I have set before you life and death, blessings and curses. Now choose life, so that you and your children may live." Choosing life means choosing to live according to God's Word.

We could look at it like this. Have you ever purchased an automobile or a washing machine? Most likely, when you made your purchase, you received an owner's manual of operating instructions. In supplying you with a manual, the manufacturer intended to spare you needless mistakes and problems in the use of your machine.

As your manufacturer, God has supplied you with a manual for your proper functioning. It's called the Bible. If you refuse to read its contents, you'll run into all kinds of trouble.

I'm reminded of the customer who called a repairman when his washing machine failed to operate. Because the customer had not read his manual, he was not aware of what to check before calling for help. When the repairman arrived, he discovered that the machine had not been plugged into the electrical outlet. He inserted the plug and wrote a substantial bill for his services.

Far worse consequences result when a person neglects to read God's manual for life.

Persistent refusal could result in eternal damnation.

Decide today to exercise your privilege of choice by choosing life. Since God made you, He knows best how you function. Trust

Him. Take His advice and base your choosing on His perfect wisdom. You won't regret it.

Determine Your Destiny

While studying abroad several years ago, I was amazed at the fatalistic mentality of the people in the country where I was living. For them, life was some thing to be taken lying down. Fate, not individual choice, determined the future.

Since then, I have discovered that this same fatalistic mentality prevails to a considerable degree throughout the world. This mentality believes that life happens to you and that you have no control over it. It can be summed up in the phrase, "Che sarà, sarà."

As a free will agent, you have within you the power to decide what your future will be. The future does not come upon you unexpectedly. You prepare for it either by decisive action or by default. Not preparing for your future is preparing for failure.

Through an act of your will, you can decide now what your future is going to be. While it is true that some situations may occur that will be beyond your control, it is also true that you can determine now whether you will allow those situations to affect you positively or negatively.

We've already discussed goal-setting, a crucial part of determining your destiny. The Word of God says, "We should make plans—counting on God to direct us" (Proverbs 16: 9 TLB). Planning for the future is God's will for your life. If you don't make specific plans for your future, you won't like where you'll end up.

When Jesus came to earth, He had a specific plan. It was to give His life as a ransom for us so that we might live. Never once did Jesus take His eyes off His goal. The Word says that "as the time drew near for his return to heaven, he moved steadily onward towards Jerusalem with an iron will" (Luke 9: 51 TLB, Italics mine).

Along the way, Jesus set specific goals to teach in certain places, to train His disciples, and to minister to the sick. He always had a plan of action. You too need a plan of action. In developing one, you will be imitating Jesus, and you will be moving one step closer to becoming great.

Freedom to Be Creative

Because you are made in the image of God, you have within you a magnificent urge to create. This creative urge is a great gift which God intends for you to develop for His glory, for the furthering of His kingdom, and for your personal fulfillment.

In Jesus you have received the fullness of God Himself (Colossians 2: 9), and with that fullness, the ability to create beyond your wildest dreams. God says in His Word that He is able to do in you exceedingly more than you could ever ask or think (Ephesians 3: 20).

One of the most exciting revelations I have ever received through God's Word is the realization that as long as I am rooted and grounded in Him, I am free to do anything I choose. Because I am in love with the Lord, I would never deliberately choose to do anything out of keeping with His will. With God's Word as my spiritual parameter, I am free to determine my destiny according to the desires of my heart. If my heart is in love with God, then my desires will be His desires and His desires will be mine.

If you are in Christ Jesus, those creative ideas that gently drop into your mind at the most unexpected times are creative gems straight from the mind of God. Don't let them get away. God wants you to do something with them.

I keep a notebook in my purse, in my car, and at my bedside so that I can immediately jot down the myriad ideas that God drops into my spirit every day. Later that day or that week, I take all of my ideas and place them in my "Idea File." So far, God has given me enough ideas for several lifetimes.

You too can receive ideas from God if you are open to them. The Bible says that God is the Author of witty inventions, or clever ideas (Proverbs 8: 12). If you need a new idea for your business, just ask God to give you one. As a Christian, you are in Christ, and the Word says that "in Him lie hidden all the mighty, untapped treasures of wisdom and knowledge" (Colossians 2: 3 TLB). You have the right to tap into that reservoir of wisdom and knowledge and draw what you need to fulfill the desires of your heart.

Exercise your creativity. It is part of the privilege of choice which God has so graciously given to you. As you respond to the creative urge within you, you will be amazed at what you will accomplish.

Chapter Eighteen

The Responsibility of Choice

Not only is choice a privilege; it is also a responsibility. Inherent in the gift of choice is the responsibility to use it according to the guidelines set forth by God in His Word.

Because many of our choices affect the lives of others, we must make them with wisdom. When you face difficult choices, here are some points to keep in mind:

1) What does the Word of God say about the decision you are facing? If there is no specific direction, what Scriptural principle can you apply to your particular situation?

2) Will your decision draw you closer to God or away from Him?

3) How will your choice affect your immediate family, your church family, your co-workers?

4) Are you willing to stand by your choice once it is made?

Someone once said that you win or lose by the way you choose. Being responsible in your choices is the mark of a giant. Making responsible choices will not only sell you on you; it will sell others on you too.

Eagles and Crabs

Of all the birds of the air, the eagle holds the place of highest honor. Flying at altitudes where no other bird will fly, he penetrates the swift jet airflows that other birds will never know. His position of height gives him a panoramic view of the earth below, while at the same time it allows him to experience the tranquility of solitude in the rarefied heavens. Content to fly alone, the eagle separates himself from the crowd to pursue the majestic purpose for which he was created.

Of all birds, the eagle is the most like God and the most like man. His life reflects the dignity and grandeur of a creature born for greatness.

The crab, on the other hand, is an earth-bound creature. Because he lives at much lower altitudes, his sights are lower. While the eagle delights in nonconformity, the crab tends to be a conformist. Eagles fly into the sun, but crabs crawl into the sand.

The Tug of Mediocrity (The Crab Story)

In southern New Jersey where I grew up, crabbing is a popular sport. The bay area is full of crabs, and during my teen years, I would join my friends for a fun-filled afternoon of crabbing.

Once the crabs are caught, they are placed in a box where an interesting phenomenon occurs. As long as there is only one crab in the box, he will try to climb out and escape. But as soon as a second crab is placed in the box, he will immediately grab hold of the first crab's legs and start to pull him back into the box. When there are several crabs in the box, there is a continual fight to keep any crabs from escaping.

Most people are like crabs. Whenever someone tries to break out of the mold of mediocrity, the "committee of they" will be close by, eager to thwart his efforts.

Perhaps it has already happened to you. You've been offered an opportunity to go into business for yourself, but your best friend said you'd never make it in this economy. You've decided to go to college at age fifty-two, but your family says you're too old.

Few of us have escaped criticism for trying to better ourselves. Criticism is cheap and flows readily from the mouths of losers. The real winners, however— those who go after their dreams and achieve them—will never criticize you. Like the eagle, they resist the tug of mediocrity exerted upon them by the crabs of the world. They choose instead to fly high into the realms of success.

Are you an eagle or a crab? You choose which you will be. Choose to be an eagle and discover your greatness.

Fighting the Status Quo

A wise man once observed that if you want to succeed in life, study the masses and do the opposite. The *status quo* in any society represents the masses of people who contentedly flow with the crowd, pulled along by the prevalent current of thought and behavior. They lack the courage and the conviction to hold on to their dreams and take, instead, the path of least resistance.

You can recognize *status-quoers* by comments like "We've been doing it this way for twenty-five years. Why change now?" Or, "Let's quit spending so much money on the space program. We don't belong in space anyway." Such primitive thinking hinders progress and causes people to die without singing their song.

Nothing is so tragic as to miss God's purpose for your life. In order to find it, you must be willing to fight the *status quo* and to follow the drumbeat of your Maker. You must be willing to swim upstream, to come out of the crowd, and to be true to yourself. As someone once said, "If you want to lead the orchestra, you must turn your back on the crowd and face the music."

Fighting the *status quo* involves a willingness to face ridicule, rejection, and criticism. It means being thick-skinned enough to allow the negative to roll off your back, while at the same time being sensitive enough to serve the very ones who are trying to hurt you.

Resist the crabs of the world. Decide to fly with the eagles. Decide to succeed!

Success Breeds Success

"Nothing succeeds like success." So goes the famous saying. Studies have shown, for example, that people who have developed a success pattern in their lives are more likely to repeat that pattern than those who continually fail. Why? Because of the law of use.

The law of use simply states that the more you use something—such as a talent, a muscle, a principle—the stronger it becomes. Therefore, the more you use success principles, the more you will reap success. And the more you reap success, the better you will be programmed to succeed.

Giants understand the law of use and make it work for them. If you want to develop a pattern of success in your life, learn and apply the principles of success that you have been discovering in this book. Use the talents God has given you. Begin right where you are. Your first attempts need not be large-scale. In fact, the Word warns us against despising small beginnings (Zechariah 4: 10). As you succeed on a small scale, you will learn how to believe God for greater successes.

Exhorting One Another

"No man is an island" wrote John Donne. And no one ever achieved success without the help of other people. Zig Ziglar often says, "You can get everything in life you want if you help enough other people get what they want."

Part of the responsibility of becoming a giant is helping others to become giants too. The Bible commands us to encourage one another daily (Hebrews 3: 13) so that God may be glorified through our lives. Then we shall know the blessings of success.

Here are some practical ways in which you can encourage others to become all that God wants them to be:

1) Observe the Golden Rule in all of your dealings with people. Treat others as you would like to be treated.

2) Always look for the good in others. Even the most cantankerous person has some good quality.

3) Compliment every person you meet. Always be sincere in your compliments.

4) Greet everyone with a smile. A smile conveys the message that you acknowledge that person as someone of worth, a fellow human being.

5) Be a good listener. The giant in life knows how to focus his attention on the other person and to listen with his heart. Listening with your heart gives the other person a sense of importance and a feeling that you really care.

6) Pray for those whom God brings to your mind. Encouraging one another through prayer is one of the most powerful ways of helping others to reach their full potential in Christ.

Chapter Nineteen

The Power of Choice

The power inherent in choice can literally change the course of history. Choice has a ripple effect. The choices we make can affect the lives of people we will never meet.

Let's consider, for example, our right to vote. The power we exercise in choosing our candidates will affect not only the people of our generation but those of generations to come.

Likewise, if you are a parent, the choices you make in rearing your children will profoundly affect your descendants in significant ways.

Let me illustrate from my own life. Shortly before the outbreak of World War I, my paternal grandfather made the decision to leave his Italian homeland to emigrate to the United States. Like so many dreamers of his day, he longed for an opportunity to better himself and his family. He found in this land the wonderful freedom to prosper financially and thus provide for his family those benefits that he himself had lacked as a child.

My grandfather's decision to come to America has directly and profoundly affected my life. It is because of his choice to follow his dream that I have been able to follow my dreams in a country where dreams abound and where opportunity is unlimited.

Your power of choice reflects God's great love for you. In giving us the power to choose, God took the greatest risk possible—the risk of our choosing to reject Him. Had He made us robots, we would not be able to love Him freely. But when we choose to love Him, then our love is genuine.

Use your power of choice wisely. Give prayerful thought to your decisions. Remember that one single person can change the entire world.

The One Factor

The evening activities were fast coming to a close in the huge auditorium where I had just participated in an exciting motivational meeting. Ushers were quickly distributing candles to each person present in preparation for the traditional candlelight ceremony.

As the main speaker asked us to stand, the house lights were turned off. Total darkness settled across the room. Then the speaker struck a match and lit his candle. How powerfully that one little candle dispelled the darkness.

The speaker then turned to his wife standing next to him and lit her candle. One by one, each candle was lit, and soon the entire auditorium was filled with light. The resulting sight was truly inspiring.

Jesus said, "You are the light of the world" (Matthew 5: 14 NIV). If you don't shine your light, there will be darkness in your corner of the world. A person doesn't light his candle to put it under a bushel. He puts it on a lampstand so that others may be brightened by its light.

In order for you to achieve greatness, you must see yourself as a light to a lost and hurting world. If you are a Christian, then you have within you the light that the world needs.

Don't put yourself down because you are only one person—only one light. It took only one little candle to dispel the darkness in that auditorium. So it is with you. See yourself as one light in the world of darkness that immediately surrounds you. One light in a room full of darkness will always overcome the darkness.

This hurting world needs the light that only you can give. Only you can shine your light. If you don't shine it, it simply won't shine. Yes, you are only one person, but as you give your light to others, you will be multiplying yourself throughout the world. By duplicating your light in others, you will have tapped into the secret of achieving greatness.

You Can Change the World

Margo passed through my life for a brief two hours. Yet the impact she made on me in that short period of time has had eternal consequences not only for her and for me, but for all with whom I have shared the message of salvation which she so graciously offered me.

When I met Margo, I was a self-centered, self-righteous, young intellectual bent on going my own way. Having been brought up in a traditional, mainline church, I considered myself religious. In reality, I had a form of godliness but not the power thereof (II Timothy 3: 5 KJV).

Despite my initial rejection of Margo's message, I was deeply impressed by the power of her love. That love was to bear fruit three years later when, through a series of subsequent events, I finally accepted Jesus Christ into my heart as my personal Savior and Lord.

Margo was only one person, but she made a big difference. Because of her, the world is being changed as her influence, multiplied through me, is reaching far and wide.

Like Margo, you too can change the world. You too can be a giant for Jesus. Giants put no limits on God but realize that through Christ they can do all things.

If you're thinking *What difference can I make?*, then you need to work on your self-image. You need to dig into the Word of God to discover who you really are in Christ. When you make that discovery, nothing will be able to hold you back.

You are important! If you weren't, God would not have created you. He created you because He wants you to have fellowship with Him and to do a special work in the earth. No one else can fulfill your calling in exactly the same way that you can fulfill it. God has equipped you with precisely the right talents, the right characteristics, and the right temperament to do the job He has called you to do.

Stop looking at yourself as just another cog in the wheel. Begin looking at yourself as an important cog in the wheel. If one cog is missing, the wheel can't turn properly. So too with the

Body of Christ. If you're not fulfilling your calling, then the Body can't function as it should.

Remember that you and God are a majority in any situation. Jesus was only one Person, but look at His impact on the world. As His heir, you are now walking in His shoes. Your impact should be equal to His for He said, "In solemn truth I tell you, anyone believing in me shall do the same miracles I have done, and even greater ones, because I am going to be with the Father" (John 14: 12 TLB). If Jesus believes so much in you, how can you not believe in yourself?

Determine to put aside the doubt that so easily assails you. Stop tearing yourself down through negative self-talk. Instead, start telling yourself that you can make a difference. With God's help, you can change the world.

Chapter Twenty

The Fruit of Choice

At age fifty-two, Ed found himself jobless and penniless. Because of an outburst of anger toward his boss, he had been fired from his position as office manager for a retail store.

This wasn't the first time that Ed had lost a job because of his bad temper. Through the years, he had developed a reputation for being hot-headed and inflexible. As a result, others found it very difficult to work with him. Moreover, whenever an opportunity for a promotion came up, Ed was always bypassed.

At one time, a caring employer had counseled Ed about his anger, but Ed had been too proud to take the advice. Now he was reaping the consequences of his choice.

For every action, there is a reaction. Ed's action—giving in to his anger—produced a corresponding reaction—his boss fired him. But Ed's action was the direct result of a choice. When he opted for anger, he automatically chose the fruit of anger.

One of the basic lessons to be learned in pursuing greatness is that choices bear consequences. In other words, choices produce fruit. What kind of fruit you produce in your life will be determined by the choices you make.

Choose Life

Choosing life means making choices based on God's Word. When you choose according to God's Word, you will always produce good fruit. When, however, you compromise the Word in your choices, you will always produce bad fruit. Decide now that your choices will always produce good fruit.

The View from the Top

If you've ever climbed a mountain, you know the exhilarating feeling of accomplishment after the struggles of the climb. As you gaze at the great expanse below you, you joyfully breathe in the crisp, fresh, rarefied air found only in high altitudes. You feel good knowing that you've done something that most people have never done.

Because you were willing to pay the price that most people are not willing to pay, you can now experience the astounding beauty of God's creation from a vantage point unknown to those who have not made the climb. Like the eagle, you have soared to uncommon heights and, in the process, you have nurtured your self-esteem.

As with the mountain climber who sees the world from a different vantage point, so it is with the follower of Jesus Christ. He sits with Christ in heavenly places (Ephesians 2: 6) and sees life from God's viewpoint. The Christian recognizes his position of power and authority in Christ and acts in accordance with that position. Ultimately, achieving greatness means recognizing and accepting who you are in Christ and living daily according to that knowledge.

The 80-20 Rule

Statistics have repeatedly shown that in every sampling of one hundred people, only twenty will achieve success. It is an established fact that 20% of the people in the world control 80% of the wealth. Why is this so, and how can you become a part of that 20% of achievers?

Several characteristics differentiate the twenty-percenters from the eighty-percenters. Here are the most significant:

1. *The "Why."* Twenty-percenters have a "why," a dream, a burning desire. This dream keeps them self-motivated and energizes them to achieve it.

2. *Commitment.* Twenty-percenters are committed to their dream. They are willing to pay any price—as long as it is moral and legal—to achieve it.

3. *Persistence.* Twenty-percenters never quit. They have burned all bridges behind them and move forward despite setbacks. Their eyes are constantly on their goal.

4. *Consistence.* Twenty-percenters develop a plan of action and stick to it.

5. *Courage.* Twenty-percenters are not afraid to take risks. Their philosophy is "Nothing ventured, nothing gained."

6. *Service.* Twenty-percenters have a genuine desire to serve their fellow man. They realize that true success is based on giving, and that one succeeds by helping others to succeed.

7. *Association with Successful People.* Twenty-percenters sharpen their wits on the wits of other successful people. They know they will become like the people with whom they associate.

8. *Understanding of Success Principles.* Twenty-percenters have discovered and continually apply God's success principles. They are always growing and learning. Their lives are characterized by balance and peace.

Cream still rises to the top. By incorporating the above characteristics into your life, you too can be a twenty-percenter. You too can be the winner that God made you to be.

Run with the Winners

In his best-selling book, *The Winner's Edge* (Berkley Books, 1980, p. 16), Dr. Denis Waitley describes winners as "those individuals who in a very natural, free-flowing way seem to consistently get what they want from life by providing valuable service to others." Undoubtedly, you've met some people who seem to have everything going for them, who attract success at every turn and with seemingly no effort on their part.

What is it that makes such people tick? As you've learned so far, winners are winners because they choose to be winners. Surprisingly, however, they stand out from the rest of the crowd by only a slight margin.

There is a difference of only one degree between hot water and boiling water. Likewise, many a race has been won by a margin of only a microsecond. It is usually only this slight margin that distinguishes a winner from one who is not.

A wrestling friend of mine once recounted to me his most challenging match. A champion himself, he was defeated by an opponent whose only edge was an extra reserve of air. Obviously, the winning wrestler was in slightly better shape, the result of perhaps only a few extra hours of training.

And so it is with winners in every area of life. The winner is the person who gets up an hour earlier than most people to pray and to plan his day. He is the person who does one more push-up, no matter how much it hurts, or who writes one more sentence, even though he is about to collapse on his typewriter. The winner is that person who is willing to hang in there when the going gets rough, the one who is willing to go the extra mile to help a friend.

Being a winner is not a matter of talent but of attitude. Winners keep their eye on the goal without counting the cost of the sacrifice. They are willing to trade convenience for success and cost for value. They realize that true happiness lies not in reaching the goal but in pursuing it.

Winners have discovered a worthwhile purpose in life and are excited about fulfilling it. They take their past—no matter what it was—and use it to create a positive future. They do not fear failure, yet they always expect success.

No matter what your life has been up to this point, you can choose to run with the winners.

Here's how:

1. *Refuse to allow the negative experiences of your past to influence your future in a negative way.* The story is told of twin brothers who grew up with an alcoholic father. In later life, one of the twins also became an alcoholic while the other never touched any kind of alcoholic drink. When the brothers were asked why they had turned out the way they had, both of them replied, "What else could we have done with a father like ours?" Your past can be a blessing or a bane. It will be in your life whatever you allow it to be.

2. *Whatever you choose to do in life, put forth your best effort—and more.* Run that extra block when you're already out of wind, make that extra call when it's time to go home, schedule that extra interview when you've just had five rejections. The Word of God says, "Whatever your hand finds to do, do it with all your might" (Ecclesiastes 9: 10 NIV).

3. *Talk to yourself only in positive terms.* When you do something well, compliment yourself. When you miss the mark, tell yourself, "That wasn't like me. I'll do better next time." We have seen that positive self-talk is a key to becoming great. If you want to run with the winners, talk to yourself like a winner.

4. *Be optimistic about life.* People who expect the best get the best. If you want to be a winner, expect to win. After talking with several winners, I found that every one of them had expected to win. Psychologists refer to this phenomenon as "the self-fulfilling prophecy." You will become what you expect to become.

5. *Commit your life to the Lord and expect Him to help you succeed.* God has a vested interest in your success. When you succeed, He is glorified as you share your reason for success with others. The Bible promises that if you commit your life to the Lord, you will succeed in whatever you do (Proverbs 16: 3).

You were made to be a winner. Get out there and win!

Part VI

The Believer's Authority

A European immigrant once made the long boat trip across the Atlantic on a meager diet of cheese and crackers. This simple man with rugged hands had had a life-long dream of starting his own business in America. After years of scrimping and saving for his trip, he finally had enough money to buy his ticket.

Throughout the voyage he kept mostly to himself, subsisting on his diet of cheese and crackers. The ship finally docked in New York Harbor, and the passengers began to disembark. The captain stood by, bidding farewell to each of his passengers. When it was time for the little European immigrant to shake the captain's hand, the captain remarked, "I hope your trip was a pleasant one. I was somewhat concerned because I never saw you share a meal with us in the dining room."

"Oh," replied the immigrant, "I brought along a supply of cheese and crackers because I had only enough money for my ticket and not for meals."

Genuinely grieved, the captain responded, "But your meals were included in the price of the ticket!"

How many of us Christians are like this poor immigrant? We go through life enduring inferiority, sickness, and financial lack, totally unaware that the blessings of self-esteem, health, and prosperity are included in the price Christ paid for our ticket to salvation.

Before the fall of Adam and Eve, man ruled the earth. In Genesis 1: 27-28 NIV we read:

> So God created man in his own image, in the image of God he created him; male and female he created them. God blessed them and said to them, "Be fruitful and increase in number; fill the earth and subdue it. Rule over the fish

of the sea and the birds of the air and over every living creature that moves on the ground.

Through disobedience, man forfeited his rulership over the earth to Satan. But the glorious news of the Gospel of Jesus Christ is that, through accepting His redemptive work on Calvary, we can once again have that dominion over the earth that God originally intended for us to have. We can once again exercise our God-given authority and reclaim the world for Christ.

Chapter Twenty-One

It's War!

Being born again gives you the right to resume your place of authority in God's kingdom. Through Jesus Christ, you have regained power over the enemy. But Satan, of course, doesn't like this. Consequently, until the return of Jesus, your life on this earth will be characterized by spiritual warfare. The great news, however, is that the battle has already been won. The last chapter has already been written. All that is required of you is that you stand fast, relying totally on the Word of God. If you do so, when the winds of battle subside, you will still be standing.

But how do you keep on standing in the midst of the battle? What do you as a Christian need to know about the enemy and how he operates?

First of all, you need to know who the enemy is. Basically, there are only two spiritual forces at work in the world today: the force of God and the force of Satan. Scripture refers to these two forces as the spirit of Christ and the spirit of Anti-Christ. These forces are continually at war with each other for the spirit of man. Their battleground is the mind of man.

You learned in an earlier chapter of the importance of renewing your mind according to the Word of God. Why? Because the only place that Satan can fight you is in your mind. It is there that he plants his seeds of death and destruction. If you allow these negative seeds to take root, they will infiltrate your spirit and your body. If, however, you immediately recognize Satan for who he is—the arch-deceiver and the father of lies—then you can instantly destroy his seeds before they have an opportunity to take root.

How can you destroy negative seeds before they take root? Here are some proven guidelines:

1) Become a diligent student of the Word of God so that you will be able readily to distinguish between good seed and bad seed. If you do not continually feed on the Word, you will not be able to tell the difference between truth and error.

Satan packages his seeds in light. From the outside they look good, but on the inside they are rotten.

A bank teller does not learn how to recognize counterfeit money by handling it. On the contrary, he handles only real money. As a result, he becomes so accustomed to the feel and the look of real money that he instantly recognizes a counterfeit.

So it is with us. As we handle God's Word day by day and internalize its truths, we will immediately recognize anything that contradicts it. Falsehood will instantly sound an alarm in our spirits, and we will be able to destroy that bad seed before it takes root.

2) Recognize that just as God has His ministering angels whose purpose it is to assist the saints (Hebrews 1: 14), so does Satan have his cohort of evil spirits whose purpose it is to wreak havoc in the earth. As believers in Jesus Christ, we have the authority to use the Name of Jesus to cast out these evil spirits and to tear down their strongholds in our lives and in the lives of others.

Principalities and Powers in High Places

Have you ever noticed that certain areas of a country are characterized by particular moral problems? For instance, homosexuality is especially rampant in one area while greed rages in another. Why is this so? For the simple reason that certain demonic spirits operate with greater authority in some geographical areas than in others.

While it is not the purpose of this book to discuss demonology, it is important in the process of pursuing greatness that you be aware of the forces fighting to tear you down. These forces are spiritual in nature, and the only way to combat them is through the use of spiritual weapons.

Ephesians 6: 12 KJV warns us of the nature of our battle: "For we wrestle not against flesh and blood, but against principalities, against powers, against the rulers of the darkness of this world, against spiritual wickedness in high places." What are these principalities and powers, these rulers of darkness and spiritual wickedness in high places? They are the demon hordes, in varying order of rank, that Satan has assigned to destroy you.

The word "principalities" indicates that there are certain areas over which particular demonic princes rule. To a great extent, these areas involve politics and government since these represent the key authority structure in the lives of the people.

What Scriptural proof do we have of the existence of these ruler princes? Let's take a look at Daniel 10: 12- 14 TLB. The Angel of the Lord is speaking:

> Don't be frightened, Daniel, for your request has been heard in heaven and was answered the very first day you began to fast before the Lord and pray for understanding; that very day I was sent here to meet you. But for twenty-one days, the mighty Evil Spirit who overrules the kingdom of Persia blocked my way. Then Michael, one of the top officers of the heavenly army, came to help me, so that I was able to break through these spirit rulers of Persia.

We see from this passage that the angel of God engaged in combat with a demonic ruler spirit which had been assigned to the kingdom of Persia.

In addition to the ruler spirits, or principalities, there are the demons of power. In his informative booklet, *The Battle in the Heavenlies* (Bible Revivals, n.d., pp. 9-10), David Nunn writes:

> These (demons of power) are demons which attack all men, Christians and non-Christians alike. They excite feelings, the imaginations, and cause men to do all kinds of vile and unclean things. They are the ones which cause divorce, hatred, jealousy; they cause people to kill, rob, betray; they bring about broken homes, church troubles,

and many other such things. Their business is to frustrate; to conquer; their business is to destroy your place in Christ.

These demons of power will attack you with all kinds of negative thoughts. But, praise God, because you are in Christ Jesus, you can send them packing. You do this by taking "captive every thought to make it obedient to Christ" (II Corinthians 10: 5 NIV). Moreover, you can rejoice that "greater is He that is in you than he that is in the world" (I John 4:4 KJV).

Enemy Tactics

The Council of Demons was having a meeting.

"We must devise a plan to cause Christians to stray from the truth," said their leader Satan.

"I know of a way," offered one demon excitedly. "We could tell them that the Bible is not the Word of God."

"They would never believe that," said Satan with a smirk.

"Well," suggested another demon, "we could tell them that Jesus Christ did not really rise from the dead."

"They wouldn't believe that either," shouted the other members of the Council.

After several moments of silence, another demon slowly began to speak. "We could attack the Christian with discouragement," he hissed.

All eyes turned to him in wondrous agreement.

"Why, of course!" exclaimed Satan with a wicked smile. "That is a brilliant idea! The Christian would never suspect that we would use such a tactic. I do believe that it will produce marvelous results."

And with that, the Council of Demons burst into riotous laughter.

Perhaps you, like me, have been the Christian targeted in the above story. At some point in our lives, all of us have faced discouragement. Discouragement results from deception which is false perception.

Satan's chief tool is deception. If he can get you to accept a lie as true, then he has you. This is exactly what happens to you when you get down on yourself.

All of your life you may have heard that you were a failure, that you would never do anything great, that you were destined to mediocrity. All of those statements were lies that you accepted as truth. Selling yourself on you involves differentiating between the lies you were fed and the truth which God declares about you in His Word.

Closely connected with deception is fear, another common tactic used by the enemy. We mentioned in an earlier chapter that fear stands for "false evidence appearing real." Once again, the lie is at the basis of Satan's game plan.

What will you choose to believe today? The lies which Satan has spoken through others to destroy you, or the truth of God's Word which says that you are more than a conqueror through Christ (Romans 8: 37)?

Remember: Satan goes around as a roaring lion seeking whom he may devour. The Bible doesn't say he is a roaring lion. When you realize the authority you have in Christ, Satan won't stand a chance in your life. He'll tremble every time he sees you coming.

Chapter Twenty-Two

Preparing for Battle

Just as a soldier must go through basic training before he can fight, so we Christians must be trained before we can face the enemy.

In His wisdom and mercy, God has totally provided for our training through His Word. Moreover, He has supplied us with apostles, evangelists, prophets, pastors, and teachers who serve as our instructors in God's basic training program.

Basic Training

When a person enlists in a branch of the armed services, he officially becomes a member of the military with all of the responsibilities and privileges attached to that position. Although he is officially a member of the armed services, however, he still has to be trained in order to develop the fighting potential within him. Being in the military does not automatically make him an expert soldier.

The same is true of the Christian. Although legally and officially a member of the army of Christ, he must be trained in spiritual warfare so that he can stand against the attacks of the enemy. This training comes through hearing the Word of God and applying it to every circumstance of life.

Putting On Your Armor

Once trained, the Christian is ready to put on his armor and go to war. Let's look at a description of this armor in the sixth chapter of the Book of Ephesians, verses 10-19 NIV:

> Finally, be strong in the Lord and in his mighty power. Put on the full armor of God so that you can take your stand

against the devil's schemes. For our struggle is not against flesh and blood, but against the rulers, against the authorities, against the powers of this dark world and against the spiritual forces of evil in the heavenly realms. Therefore put on the full armor of God, so that when the day of evil comes, you may be able to stand your ground, and after you have done everything, to stand. Stand firm then, with the belt of truth buckled around your waist, with the breastplate of righteousness in place, and with your feet fitted with the readiness that comes from the gospel of peace. In addition to all this, take up the shield of faith, with which you can extinguish all the flaming arrows of the evil one. Take the helmet of salvation and the sword of the Spirit, which is the word of God. And pray in the Spirit on all occasions with all kinds of prayers and requests. With this in mind, be alert and always keep on praying for all the saints.

Each part of the armor represents a spiritual attitude which you as a Christian must maintain in order to achieve greatness. Let's examine each part of the armor more closely.

1. *The belt of truth.* This part of the armor represents the Word of God. As Kenneth Hagin writes in his book, *The Believer's Authority* (Faith Library Publications, 1984, p. 53), "Like a soldier's belt, it holds the rest of the armor in place."

2. *The breastplate of righteousness.* This represents your right-standing in God through Jesus Christ.

3. *Feet fitted with the readiness that comes from the gospel of peace.* Your shod feet represent your availability and faithfulness in spreading the Gospel message.

4. *The shield of faith.* In medieval days, the shield covered the entire body. The shield of faith represents your total safety in Christ where the enemy's fiery darts cannot touch you.

5. *The helmet of salvation.* This represents your hope that Christ will protect you from falling into error.

6. *The sword of the Spirit.* This part of your armor represents the Word of God. Whereas all the other parts are used defensively, the sword of the Spirit is to be used offensively. Whenever Satan comes against you in any way, take the sword of the Word of God and pierce him with it.

Having put on the whole armor of God, you are now ready to engage in battle. But, unlike any earthly battle, you already know the outcome of your spiritual battle. Satan, your foe, has already been defeated by the blood of Christ. The battle is no longer yours; it is the Lord's (I Samuel 17:47).

Knowing this, you can boldly enter the fray, confident that if you stand firm, you will surely win. For "no weapon that is formed against you shall prosper" (Isaiah 54: 17 AMP). How exciting it is to know that as long as we hold fast to God's promises in His Word, we will always emerge victorious.

God wants you to realize who you are in Him. He doesn't want you to live a defeated life any longer. You were made for greatness in this world and in the world to come. But you will never achieve that greatness until you discover who you really are in Christ. You are the child of a King, and the keys of the Kingdom have been placed in your hands.

Chapter Twenty-Three

The Keys of the Kingdom

Have you ever wondered about the significance of keys? Keys represent authority. They allow you entrance into areas restricted to others. Keys give you selective access to information, to things, and to people.

When Jesus died and confronted Satan on his own turf, He took back the keys of authority that Satan had stolen from Adam and Eve. But not only did Jesus take back those keys; He handed them over to you and me.

Because you now hold the keys to God's Kingdom, you have free access at anytime to the throne room of God Himself. There you can bare your heart, ask His forgiveness, and discuss any need.

With the privilege of holding the keys to the Kingdom of God comes the responsibility to use them wisely. Two of these keys have special significance in your program of selling yourself on you. They are the key of binding and loosing and the key to God's powerhouse of blessings.

The Principle of Binding and Loosing

As a follower of Jesus Christ, you have been given the authority to reclaim the earth for Him. One of the ways you exercise this authority is through the principle of binding and loosing.

In Matthew 16: 19 NIV Jesus says, "I will give you the keys of the kingdom of heaven; whatever you bind on earth will be bound in heaven, and whatever you loose on earth will be loosed in heaven." The Amplified translation makes this principle even clearer: "I will give you the keys of the kingdom of heaven, and whatever you bind—that is, declare to be improper and unlawful—on earth must be already bound in heaven; and whatever you loose on earth—declare lawful—must be what is already loosed in heaven."

There is no inferiority, sickness, or poverty in heaven. Likewise, there should be no inferiority, sickness, or poverty for those who live in the Kingdom of God in this earth.

The Kingdom of God is within you. Therefore, whatever has been bound from that Kingdom has been bound from you. By the same token, whatever has been loosed into that Kingdom—health, joy, prosperity—has also been loosed into your life through the shed blood of Jesus Christ.

Because Jesus has given you the keys of the Kingdom, you have the authority to bind from your life anything that contradicts the Word of God. You also have the power to loose into your life all that agrees with the Word of God.

God's Word says that you are to be successful, healthy, prosperous, and joyful. You are to experience and enjoy the abundant life that Jesus promised to all those who follow Him (John 10: 10). But in order to experience that abundant life, you need to know how to unlock God's powerhouse of blessings.

Unlocking God's Powerhouse

Several years ago, a terrible storm struck our area. Although New Jersey is not prone to tornadoes, this certainly looked like one to me. Having lived in Kansas for a while, I had experienced a few twisters.

During the storm, we lost all electrical power in our home. We later learned that some wires in our neighborhood had been knocked down by the high winds. Until the Electric Company got us plugged back into the powerhouse, we had to survive with candles.

Although we experienced a temporary interruption in electrical power, the source of that power was always available had we been able to unlock it. But because the connection between the wires and the power source had been broken, the power was not forthcoming. Once the connection was re-established, we had power again.

God too has a powerhouse of blessings that He is just waiting to pour out on you. But unless you know about the powerhouse and how to unlock it, you'll never enjoy what's in there for you.

A story is told of a man who died and went to heaven. When he arrived, Peter gave him a guided tour of the premises.

They came to a warehouse filled with marvelous gifts. The man saw packages marked

Health, *Financial Freedom*, and *Positive Mental Attitude*. "What are all these?" the man asked Peter.

"These are the blessings that you were meant to have on earth, but that you never claimed," replied Peter.

Quite surprised, the man exclaimed, "But I didn't know they were available to me." "Neither do a lot of Christians," Peter remarked sadly.

If your rich uncle dies and leaves you a million dollars, that money will do you no good unless you know about it and claim it. The same is true of God's blessings. Unless you are willing to claim them in faith, knowing that they rightfully belong to you because of your covenant with God through Christ, they will never be yours.

Unless you know and truly believe that Christ took away all sickness from you through the stripes He bore (I Peter 2: 24), you will never experience divine health. Unless you know and truly believe that Jesus became poor so that you through his poverty might become rich (II Corinthians 8: 9), you will never experience financial prosperity. Unless you know and truly believe that Jesus became a curse to redeem you from the curse (Galatians 3: 13), you will never know true success.

When I first began to learn about all that God had for me through the death and resurrection of Christ, it seemed too good to be true. My brain would short-circuit at the truth that such wonderful blessings were available to me today.

But, through diligent study of God's Word, I saw that these blessings are available to all believers today. And you can share in them by believing that they are for you and by claiming them for yourself through faith.

In God's powerhouse of blessings is a great self-image for you. God wants to help you become great. He has a great stake in your life and in your success. After all, He gave His Son for you.

Your success makes God more believable to those who don't know Him. When they see you succeed, they will ask you how you've done it. Then you can tell them about Jesus.

While driving down the road one day, I happened to get behind a rusted and rotting automobile with a bumper sticker proclaiming Jesus. I joyfully acknowledged a brother in Christ, but, at the same time, my heart sank for two reasons. First of all, this precious brother was obviously not aware that God had something better in store for him in terms of a car. God did not intend for him to drive around in such a battered vehicle.

Secondly, I grieved when I thought of the poor witness this believer was giving with his car. It was certainly not a testimony to God's ability to take care of His own.

God's people are destroyed for lack of knowledge of who they are in Christ (Hosea 4: 6). Don't be ignorant of your covenant with God. Get into the Word and find out what belongs to you as a follower of Jesus Christ.

Remember: your failure does not glorify God. Your success does. You were meant to unlock God's powerhouse of blessings. There are packages there waiting to be delivered to you. As long as you obey God, you have only to claim those packages and ask for their delivery.

God delights in sending you His packages of blessings. Give Him pleasure by receiving all that He wants to give you.

Chapter Twenty-Four

Possessing the Land

Claiming in faith is the key to receiving from God. When Joshua led the Israelites into the Promised Land, God told them to claim it for their inheritance.

To claim means to assume ownership. Webster lists this definition: "to assert in the face of possible contradiction." Satan will certainly attempt to contradict you as you make your claims to the blessings in God's powerhouse. But remember: Satan is the father of lies and he can speak nothing but lies. Moreover, because he is a counterfeit, his target is always the real. So, if you are undergoing an attack from the enemy, realize that what he is attacking is the truth of God in you. That truth says that you are saved, healed, and prosperous.

Our approach to Satan must be offensive. After all, he is on our turf. This earth was given to us by God, and we are to have dominion over it.

For too long, we Christians have allowed Satan to walk all over us. It's time to take the offensive for, if we resist him, he will surely flee (James 4: 7). Let's reclaim our territory from him. Here's how.

Spearheading the Attack

First of all, we need to realize that our authority over Satan is backed by the very authority of God Himself. As Kenneth Hagin points out: "God Himself is the power behind our authority! The devil and his forces are obliged to recognize our authority!" (*The Believer's Authority*, p. 7). Once we realize that God Himself is backing us in our attack against the enemy, we can face Satan without fear.

Unfortunately, many Christians are intimidated by Satan. Instead of taking an offensive approach toward him, they timidly point a toe in his direction and, when he roars, they immediately retreat. Such an attitude is destructive.

Satan should be trembling at you—not the other way around. When he comes against you, take the sword of the Word of God and drive him away from you.

You need to be aggressive when dealing with Satan. He fears you because of Jesus Who indwells you. But he will try to trick you into fearing him. If you fall for his lie, then you've lost the battle.

Satan uses the same trick to make you feel inferior. When you feel inferior, you're no match for anyone. You feel like a loser, you think like a loser, and you act like a loser. And Satan is in the business of making losers because losers don't have the courage to resist him.

If Satan can convince you that you are a loser, he won't have to fear any challenges from your camp. But when you stand up and take authority over him, and hold your ground, you can be sure that he'll run from you.

Act like the winner you really are in Christ. Put on your armor, take your sword, and meet the enemy head on.

Invading the Impossible

The fight of faith is a fight into the impossible. It is an invasion into the camp of the unseen in order to make it seen.

What impossible situation are you facing today? Have you just gone bankrupt with no source of income in sight? Has your wife just left you for another man? Or has your son just been arrested for selling drugs? Whatever impossible situation you're facing, there is a solution.

God may not always give you a way out, but He will always give you a way through. That way is prayer.

In his magnificent book, *Prayer Is Invading the Impossible* (Bridge Publishing, Inc., 1972, p. 5), Pastor Jack Hayford writes: " ... there is a way to face impossibility. Invade it. Not with a big speech of high hopes. Not in anger. Not with resignation. Not through stoical self-control. But with violence. And prayer provides the vehicle for this kind of violence."

We don't usually think of prayer and violence as going hand in hand. Yet the kind of prayer that makes things happen is that aggressive prayer that recognizes our authority in Jesus Christ and makes use of that authority. When you know who you are in Christ, you will be able to pray this kind of prayer.

Becoming great involves invading the impossible—those areas of your personality where there seems to be no hope for change—and boldly declaring that you will defy all odds by changing. It involves the courage to hope against all hope (Romans 4: 18) and to call things that are not as though they were (Romans 4: 17).

Decide to invade the impossible in your life. And once you have invaded, occupy.

Occupation Forces

When American troops entered Europe during World War II, they not only invaded, they also occupied. To occupy means "to take hold or possession of; to reside in as an owner" (Webster).

Not only are we commanded to invade Satan's territory, but we are also commanded to occupy it because it legally belongs to us. This territory includes the spiritual and mental realms as well as the physical.

Your self-image belongs to God. If Satan has robbed you of a positive self-image, reclaim it in the Name of Jesus. You have a legal right to it because of your redemption through Christ. Fight the fight, possess your healthy self-image, and stand firm as you occupy that area of your life.

When the Israelites entered the Promised Land, they had many battles to fight in order to possess the land. When the battles were won, however, they could occupy the land. That is, they could stand in dominion over it and get on with the business of doing the Lord's work.

In Luke 19: 13 KJV, Jesus says, "Occupy till I come." Not only does this mean that we should be busy working for the Lord until He comes; it also means that we are to stand fast in our authority and dominion over the earth.

How are we to do this? Through love.

Ruling in Love

The Bible calls love "the royal law" (James 2: 8). "Royal" means having to do with kings.

As kings in the earth under the Lordship of Jesus Christ, we are called to rule in love. Since God is love, this means that we are to rule in God, thinking as He would think, speaking as He would speak, and acting as He would act. But in order to rule in love, we must first love ourselves, for we cannot give what we do not have.

Having healthful love and appreciation for yourself is absolutely essential if you want to rule in love. The person who does not love himself cannot love others because he is too much concerned with his own hurts and inadequacies. He cannot see beyond his own pain to the pain of others.

God's way is to bring you to an awareness of how precious you are in His sight so that you can help others to realize how precious they too are in His sight. Dave Grant has said, "The true success of our lives will not be judged by those who admire us for our accomplishments, but by those who attribute their wholeness to our loving them, by those who have seen their true beauty and worth in our eyes" (*The Ultimate Power*, p. 19).

God created you with self-worth. The shed blood of Jesus Christ attests to that fact. When you accept Christ, you accept self-worth. And you accept Love Himself. All that remains, then, is for you to release that love that already resides within you. But you won't be able to release it until you sell yourself on you.

If you're having trouble loving, you haven't yet totally sold yourself on you.

Psychologist Alfred Adler has said that "all human failure is the result of a lack of love." If you see yourself as a failure, then you do not love yourself.

Failure is the result of fear. Success, however, is the result of love because love never fails (I Corinthians 13: 8 NIV). This doesn't mean that there won't be setbacks. But to the person who loves, setbacks are not failures but steppingstones.

There is a direct correlation between faith and love. The Bible says that faith works by love (Galatians 5: 6). If your faith doesn't seem to be working, examine how you are loving.

People fail to love because of fear. Perfect love casts out fear (I John 4: 18). If there is fear in your life, then you are not yet mature in love.

Pursuing greatness is the process of growing in love for yourself with the purpose of growing in love for others. When you love, you are acting as a channel for God to flow into another person's life.

Love is the strongest force on earth. It is best described in I Corinthians 13: 4-8 TLB:

> Love is very patient and kind, never jealous or envious, never boastful or proud, never haughty or selfish or rude. Love does not demand its own way. It is not irritable or touchy. It does not hold grudges and will hardly even notice when others do it wrong. It is never glad about injustice, but rejoices whenever truth wins out. If you love someone you will be loyal to him no matter what the cost. You will always believe in him, always expect the best of him, and always stand your ground in defending him.

Love is a decision, just as pursuing greatness is a decision. Make the decision to love. Possess the blessings that are yours when you love. When you do, you will truly be a success in life.

Part VII

Joint Heirs with Christ

When my husband and I drew up our wills, we named both of our children as joint heirs to our estate. This means that they will share equally in the fruits of our labor at the time of inheritance. Our children will have done nothing to earn this inheritance. Because of our love for them, it will simply be given to them as a free gift.

As children of the living God, we have received a free inheritance from the Father. This inheritance is made available to us through Jesus Christ.

When Jesus died and rose again from the dead, the Father gave Him all authority in heaven and earth (Matthew 28: 18). Jesus, in turn, has given that authority to us. Through Jesus, therefore, we have become joint heirs with Him in everything that the Father gave Him. We have freely received the full inheritance of the Father.

The story of the prodigal son demonstrates this truth on an earthly level (Luke 15: 11-32). Although he had sinned against his father and squandered his portion of the inheritance, the prodigal son repented and returned to his father's house. There his father welcomed him with open arms and restored him to his rightful place as heir.

Like the prodigal son, we who have returned to God by accepting Jesus Christ as Savior and Lord have been restored to our rightful place as children of God. We have become the Body of Christ.

When Christ rose from the dead, not only did His head rise but His entire body rose as well. Since we are His Body, we too rose from the dead with Him. Positionally, therefore, we are now seated with Him at the right hand of the Father. Because of our position in Christ at the right hand of the Father, we share fully in all that that position implies.

Historically, being seated at the right hand of the king implied authority. The position of Jesus, therefore, at the right hand of the Father is a position of authority. Because we are seated there with Him, it follows that we too share in His authority. We are joint heirs with Him in all the authority the Father has given Him.

Chapter Twenty-Five

Heaven Is Heir-Conditioned

The wonderful thing about the Christian message of salvation is that all who accept it share equally in the inheritance of the Father. God has no favorites (Acts 10: 34). The Kingdom of God is full of heirs who are entitled to every blessing.

But as we look around, we don't see all of our brothers and sisters sharing in the blessings to the same degree. Why not? For two reasons: lack of knowledge and lack of faith.

Far too many Christians have remained at the Cross and not gone on to the Throne. They have forgotten that Jesus not only died but that He also rose again. And it is His resurrection from the dead that is at the center of the redemption message.

The resurrection of Christ meant victory over sin, sickness, and death. As an heir of God, you share in that victory to the extent that you believe in and exercise your inherited authority. But if you are not aware of the authority you have in Christ, you cannot exercise it. Consequently, you cannot reap the blessings to which you have a legal right through Jesus Christ.

Jesus: the Second Adam

When God created Adam and Eve, He gave them authority over all the earth. He said to them:

> Multiply and fill the earth and subdue it; you are masters of the fish and birds and all the animals. And look! I have given you the seed-bearing plants throughout the earth, and all the fruit trees for your food. And I've given all the grass and plants to the animals and birds for their food (Genesis 1: 28-30 TLB).

Through sin, Adam and Eve handed over this authority to Satan. When Jesus became man, he came to earth as the second Adam. His purpose in coming was to reclaim for mankind all that Adam had forfeited to Satan. Let's look at Romans 5: 15-19 TLB:

> For this one man, Adam, brought death to many through his sin. But this one man, Jesus Christ, brought forgiveness to many through God's mercy. Adam's one sin brought the penalty of death to many, while Christ freely takes away many sins and gives glorious life instead. The sin of this one man, Adam, caused death to be king over all, but all who will take God's gift of forgiveness and acquittal are kings of life because of this one man, Jesus Christ. Yes, Adam's sin brought punishment to all, but Christ's righteousness makes men right with God, so that they can live. Adam caused many to be sinners because he disobeyed God, and Christ caused many to be made acceptable to God because he obeyed.

As the Second Adam, Jesus restored to us all that God had given to the first Adam. Jesus passed the test of obedience that Adam had failed and paid the penalty for Adam's treason. In so doing, He regained for us that authority over the earth which God had originally given to Adam and Eve. In view of what Jesus did for you, you are somebody.

Since Jesus was willing to give up His life for you, then surely you are precious in His sight. Surely you have a purpose for being. Satan will try to rob you of that purpose by telling you that you are worthless, inferior, incapable, and defeated. But God's Word emphatically proclaims the contrary.

Claim the fullness of your sonship in Jesus Christ. Take the Father at His Word and become all that He meant for you to be.

Jesus: the First-born of the Living

Did you know that, if you are a Christian, Jesus Christ is your big brother? The Word of God says that He is the first-born of many brethren (Romans 8: 29). Since Jesus is the first-born, then there must be subsequent children.

And indeed there are! All those who have accepted the substitutionary sacrifice of Christ on the Cross and His resurrection from the dead are His brothers and sisters. If you are born again, you are alive again. You are among the living who have followed in the footsteps of Jesus the Christ.

As a member of the living family of God, you are a king in the earth. Wherever you go, you should act like a king, exercising in love the authority you have through Christ. When you speak with that authority, the heavens and the earth must obey.

At its very core, achieving greatness means recognizing your kingship in Jesus Christ. It means being convinced that you truly can do all things through Christ.

It has been the Father's good pleasure to give you the keys to the Kingdom of Heaven (Luke 12: 32). What will you do with them? You can use them to reclaim your rightful inheritance from the enemy, or you can let them rust through lack of use in the drawer of ignorance and unbelief. What you decide to do with your keys will determine your success or failure in life.

Jesus: Executor of the Will of God

When you testate a will, you must indicate an executor of that will. An executor is a person who sees to it that the conditions of the will are carried out upon the death of the testator.

The will of God for mankind also needed an executor. That Executor was Jesus Christ. By His death and resurrection, He carried out the will of the Father to save mankind. And even now, He sits at the right hand of the Father as our Advocate, or Lawyer, before the judgment seat of God.

Because we are now in Christ, we too Eire executors of God's will in the earth. As the Body of Christ in the earth, we are the instruments whereby God brings about His will in the lives of men.

How do we do this? Let's take a look at what Jesus did. A close study of the Gospels reveals that Jesus carried out the will of God through the spoken word. When the sick or the demon-possessed were brought to Him, Jesus did not linger long in prayer. He did not plead with the Father for an answer to His prayers. On the contrary, Jesus spoke with authority to the sickness or to the demons and they left. He knew that His power lay in His words.

Like Jesus, we too execute the will of God through the spoken word. Just as the words of God fashioned the universe, so do our words fashion our universe.

The power of the spoken word cannot be overemphasized. You will indeed get what you say. The spoken word is the creative force which determines the course of your life (James 3: 6).

Speak right and you'll live right. Speak wrong and you'll live wrong.

I once heard of a man who was a chronic complainer. His favorite expression was, "That's a pain in the neck." I wasn't surprised when I learned that this man eventually developed a chronic pain in his neck.

Yes, what you say does matter. Choose your words carefully. Think before you speak, for with every word you utter, you are creating your future.

The demons of hell stand ready to pick up on your negative words so as to bring them to pass in your life. Likewise, the angels of God, who are sent to minister to you (Hebrews 1: 14), are ever ready to act on your positive words. Make sure your words activate angels, not demons.

The will of God is the Word of God. All of our words should line up with His Word.

As co-laborers with Christ, we are to use our words to bring about God's will in the earth. His will is that all men be saved from sin, that all men be healed, and that all men prosper in every area of their lives. Do your part in bringing God's will to pass by speaking only life-giving words.

Jesus: Our Legal Defense

It is not uncommon for wills to be contested. God's will to us, more commonly known as the New Testament, is continually being contested by the forces of hell which try to rob us of our inheritance. But those who have studied God's will know that the gates of hell cannot prevail against it (Matthew 16: 18).

When Satan accuses us, we have an Advocate before the Father in heaven. That Advocate is Jesus Himself Who acts as our Lawyer on our behalf.

Let's consider an example. The Word of God states that if you confess your sin, God is faithful and just to forgive you of that sin (I John 1: 9). After you've received your forgiveness, however, Satan may attack you with feelings of guilt about the sin. He may accuse you before the Father. But Jesus is ever ready to defend you through His promise of forgiveness in His Word.

God's promises are an integral part of His will. The Bible contains over 7000 of them which you, as a believer, have the right to claim.

Faith is the key to obtaining the promises of God. As Dr. Charles Stanley says, "When you and I begin to think the way God thinks, when we begin to see ourselves the way God sees us, we expand our capacity to receive what God has already provided for us" (*In Touch*™ Magazine, October 1984, p. 6).

This expanded capacity is expanded faith. There is only one way to receive from God, and that is through faith.

Chapter Twenty-Six

Inheriting the Promises

A father once gave his little boy a puzzle of the world to put together. On the other side of the puzzle was a picture of a man's head.

Thinking that his little son would be kept busy for quite a while, the father was surprised when the child returned after only a few moments with the entire puzzle completed.

"How did you do it so fast?" the father asked.

"Well," responded the little boy, "when I got the man's head right, the world got right."

And so it has always been. When the man gets right, the world gets right. In order for you to make your world right, you must first get yourself right with God. How do you do this? By being born again.

If you have not yet accepted Jesus Christ as your personal Savior and as the Lord of your life, I encourage you to do so now. Here is a simple prayer:

Lord Jesus, I acknowledge that You are the Christ, the Son of the Living God. I believe that You died on the Cross to save me, and that You rose again from the dead. I ask You to forgive me of all my sins, and I invite You now to come into my heart. I receive You as my Savior and as the Lord of my life. Make of me what You want me to be. In Your Name I pray. Amen.

If you prayed this prayer, you are now a child of God. You may not feel any different, but you are different. You now are a new creature. The Word says, "When someone becomes a Christian he becomes a brand new person inside. He is not the same any more. A new life has begun!" (II Corinthians 5: 17 TLB). You have been rescued out of the darkness and gloom of

Satan's kingdom and brought into the Kingdom of Light (Colossians 1: 13).

Only as a child of God can you inherit His promises. Now that you are a legal member of His family, you can claim what is yours.

In order to do this, you must learn what is yours. You do this by saturating yourself with the Word of God.

Next, you must speak the Word of God into every situation. If Satan attacks you with sickness, speak God's Word regarding healing. If Satan attacks you with financial problems, speak God's Word regarding prosperity.

And so it goes in every other area of your life. The Bible says that you shall decree a thing and it shall be established (Job 22: 28). Decree a healthy self-image and it shall be established in your life.

Chapter Twenty-Seven

The Kingdom Is Now

Are you waiting for that day when you'll reach your heavenly mansion over the hilltop? That day when Satan won't be able to harass you any longer? If you are, I have some good news for you. That day is already here.

Jesus said, "The Kingdom of God is within you" (Luke 17: 21 TLB). If you are in Christ, you don't have to wait any longer for the Kingdom of God. You're already living in it.

As a citizen of that Kingdom, you can reign over any circumstance. But how well you reign depends on how you see yourself.

More Than Conquerors

You will never achieve beyond your self-image. This principle holds true in every area of your life. Whether your challenge is losing weight or paying your bills, until you see yourself as a conqueror, you will never conquer.

Moreover, until you see yourself as a conqueror over Satan, you will never be able to withstand his attacks.

The Bible calls you not only a conqueror, but also more than a conqueror. What exactly does this mean?

We saw that a conqueror is a person who invades enemy territory and subdues the foe. When you are more than a conqueror, you not only subdue the foe, but you also reap the spoils.

When you conquer Satan, you not only conquer sin, sickness, and poverty; you also reap life, health, and prosperity. And all this through the Name of Jesus.

Blue-Blood Children

When an heir to the throne is born, he is trained and educated in all those skills that he will need to assume the throne.

Likewise, as an heir to the Kingdom of God, you too are being trained to rule in the earth. Royal blood flows through your spiritual veins. Wherever you go, you should carry yourself as Christ did when He walked the earth.

Jesus never cowered before Satan. He never retreated in the face of danger—spiritual or otherwise. On the contrary, Jesus faced every situation head-on, fully aware that He had the authority of God Himself behind Him. Even in the face of a raging storm, he took control and subdued the winds.

And so should you. As a member of the Body of Christ, you are Jesus in the world today. You are His hands, His feet, His mouth to a world lost in sin. But unless you realize who you are, you'll be ineffective in furthering God's Kingdom on earth.

God sees you as a king and a priest. Begin to see yourself as He sees you, for His image of you is the only correct one.

Get rid of that false garment of inferiority you've been wearing, and put on the royal robes of the king you really are. Take the scepter of the Word of God in your hand, and, wherever you go, decree and declare that Word.

The decree of an earthly king is law. How much more so is the decree of our heavenly King! He has decreed that you should walk in His ways and do all that He has commanded you to do. And He has commanded you to walk in the power and authority of His Son.

See yourself as Christ in the earth. When you enter a room, enter it in the Name of Jesus. When you enter a difficult situation, enter it in the Name of Jesus. Take control of negative spiritual forces in the Name of Jesus. Stand tall clothed in the mantle of the authority of God Almighty. Be the king and priest that God has declared you to be.

A Royal Priesthood

In the days of the Old Covenant, the high priest of God offered sacrifices for the atonement of sin. Only he could enter the Holy of Holies where the Presence of God dwelt. In this role, the high priest served as mediator between the people and God.

Only one man at a time served as high priest, although there were many priests who ministered before the Lord.

In the New Covenant, Jesus is our High Priest. By His death and resurrection, He atoned for our sins and mediated a reconciliation between God and man.

As brothers and sisters of Christ, we serve as royal priests in the household of God the Father, ministering to Him, worshipping Him, and furthering His Kingdom throughout the earth.

As priests of God, it is our duty and our privilege to intercede for those in need of God. We can stand in the gap for those who do not yet know God, or for those who, although born-again, have not sufficiently matured in the Christian walk to know how to receive from God.

Your call as a priest of God is to preach the message of reconciliation, the message that God is no longer angry at the world. The penalty for sin has been paid. Mankind has been set free!

That freedom is all-encompassing, for the salvation Christ earned for us was not only spiritual, but mental, physical, financial, and social as well.

Not only have you been freed from, but you have also been freed to. Freed to become all that God wants you to be.

Take up the role of priest in the service of God. Give of yourself for others through prayer.

As you do, you will be pursuing greatness.

Chapter Twenty-Eight

You Are God's Dream

Of all the dreams God ever dreamed, you are by far the greatest. When God created you, He fulfilled the deepest desire of His heart—to create a creature made in His own image and likeness, a creature who would love and serve Him forever, a creature with whom He could share His love and blessings.

Even though man, His greatest creation, betrayed Him, God never gave up on His dream. Despite a seemingly impossible setback through the fall of Adam and Eve, God went on to Plan B and got His dream back on course again through the Cross.

Imagine how God must have felt when man messed up His dream! Anyone but God would have thrown in the towel. But not God! He still believed in His man, and He was willing to pay the greatest price to salvage His dream.

How did God do it? By giving of Himself. And you too must give of yourself to fulfill your dream. Resist the voices that would try to steal your dream. Do not allow them to rob you of the joy set before you. Never give up. God never did. And aren't you glad He didn't?

Pursuing greatness means never giving up on your dream. It means holding on to it when things look the bleakest, when every glimmer of hope has faded, when night seems to be closing in on you. It means believing against all belief, hoping against all hope, and choosing to move forward even when everyone else has retreated.

Walt Disney had a dream to make people happy. Despite rejection and ridicule, he never gave up on his dream. Whenever opposition to one of his ideas was unanimous, he took it as a signal to proceed with the idea.

Today Walt Disney is a legend. His cartoon characters have delighted generations of children and their parents, and both Disneyland and Disney World have kept America young.

Without doubt, Walt Disney achieved his dream. The wealth of happiness he has brought and continues to bring to the world can never be measured. He was only one man—but he never gave up on his dream.

You too must follow your dream. Since God never gave up on you, then you must never give up on yourself.

What are you facing today that's keeping you from fulfilling your dream? Is it fear, poverty, sickness? Whatever it is, you can overcome it through the Blood of Jesus. You need only to be willing to change and to follow God's principles for success.

Whatever your dream, you can achieve it with the help of God.

The Father-Heart of God

When our first child was born, it seemed as though the whole world knew it. I suddenly found myself married to a human broadcasting system whose only news item was the exciting birth of our daughter. Nurses visited me bearing word that the entire hospital, where my husband worked as a physician, had learned of our baby's birth within minutes after the joyous event.

My husband's father-heart made its appearance that wonderful day and has grown ever since. It has revealed itself in many situations since then, displaying love, hope, comfort, correction, sympathy, compassion, encouragement, and strength. Now, several years later, he is still broadcasting good news of both of our lovely daughters.

If my husband's father-heart is so grand, how much more so is the Father-heart of God.

A very big part of pursuing greatness is coming to know God as your loving Father. Many Christians still view God as a tyrannical judge, with gavel in hand, ready to pounce on them for every wrong move. This image grieves the heart of God.

The wrath of God is stored up only for those who reject Him. His children—those who willingly receive Him—are enveloped in the cloud of His love and favor.

God's heart tends toward His children. He desires to give them every blessing. All of these blessings are wrapped up in Jesus. Through Him, we can come to know the Father.

It has been said that man began to feel inferior when he lost touch with God. You can regain that union with God by surrendering your life totally to Him through Jesus, His Son.

God knows and cares about your deepest needs. He wants you to come to Him and to pour out your heart to Him. He is always ready to listen to you and to help you.

Remember: God is in the blessings business. Approach Him with the faith of a little child approaching his loving Daddy. He's ready and willing to meet your every need.

Fishing for Men

The natural consequence of achieving greatness is a desire to reach out to other people. By raising your own self-image, you take your eyes off yourself and consider the needs of others.

Dave Grant has said that love is a channel, not a reservoir. When you achieve greatness, you recognize your responsibility to help others do the same thing.

Jesus said, "Freely you have received, freely give" (Matthew 10: 8 NIV). It is no coincidence that you have read this book. As a friend of mine would say, it is a "God-incidence."

Share what you have learned with those who still struggle with a poor self-image. Jesus has commissioned us to fish for men (Mark 1: 17; Matthew 28: 19). We are to fish for the whole man—spirit, soul, and body. In so doing, you will be unleashing a positive ripple effect whose impact in distance and time will be immeasurable.

Make your life an example of faith, hope, and love. Choose to become great so that countless others can follow in your footsteps.

About The Author

Dr. MaryAnn Diorio is a widely published, award-winning author of fiction, non-fiction, and poetry for both children and adults. Her short stories, articles, and poems have appeared in more than 100 publications, including *The Saturday Evening Post*, the *Young Generation Book of Short Stories*, and Billy Graham's *Decision* magazine. She is the author of three non-fiction books for children: *A Student's Guide to Nathaniel Hawthorne* (Enslow, 2004), *A Student's* Guide to Herman Melville (Enslow, 2006), and A Student's Guide to Mark Twain (Enslow, 2008).

Dr. MaryAnn, as she is affectionately called, recently completed her first novel for adults entitled *The Madonna of Pisano*, and her first novel for middle-grade children entitled *Dixie Randolph and the Giant of Seabury Beach*. She writes a weekly blog for writers called The Write Power.

Dr. MaryAnn is founder and president of TopNotch Communications Group, LLC, a full-service firm providing writing, coaching, and translation services to individuals and businesses around the world. TopNotch Communications Group, LLC, holds an A-Plus Rating from the New Jersey Better Business Bureau. Dr. MaryAnn is also a Certified Professional Résumé Writer (CPRW), a Certified Life Coach, and a Certified Behavioral Consultant. She holds the PhD in French with a concentration in Comparative Literature from the University of Kansas and the Doctor of Ministry in Christian Counseling from Christian Leadership University. Currently, she is completing the MFA in Writing Popular Fiction from Seton Hill University.

Dr. Diorio is founder and president of MaryAnn Diorio Ministries, a ministry designed to help set people free through the written and spoken Word of God. To relax, she loves to read, draw and paint, and play the piano.

Dr. MaryAnn currently resides in New Jersey with her wonderful husband of 41 years, Dominic, an ER physician. They are the blessed parents of two adult daughters and five rambunctious grandchildren.

Other Books by Dr. MaryAnn Diorio:

Fiction

The Italian Chronicles Trilogy
 Book 1: The Madonna of Pisano
 Book 2: A Sicilian Farewell
 Book 3: Return to Bella Terra

Surrender to Love

Magnolia Memories

A Christmas Homecoming

Children's Books

The Dandelion Patch

Toby Too Small

Candle Love

Who Is Jesus?

Do Angels Ride Ponies?

Non-Fiction

A Student's Guide to Nathaniel Hawthorne

A Student's Guide to Herman Melville

A Student's Guide to Mark Twain

From the Treadmill to the Balance Beam

Making Your Marriage Work

The ABCs of TopNotch Writing

www.ingramcontent.com/pod-product-compliance
Lightning Source LLC
Chambersburg PA
CBHW050637300426
44112CB00012B/1830